CANDLE BIBLE HANDBOOK

Published by Candle Books
an imprint of
Lion Hudson plc
Wilkinson House, Jordan Hill Road,
Oxford OX2 8DR, England
www.lionhudson.com/candle

Designer: Simon Emery
Desk editor: Abby Gough
Indexer: Christopher Pipe

ISBN 978 1 85985 586 7
e-ISBN 978 1 78128 125 3

First edition 2014

A catalogue record for this book is available
from the British Library

Printed and bound in China,
January 2014, LH23

CANDLE BIBLE HANDBOOK

by Terry Jean Day & Carol J. Smith
Edited and revised by Dr Tim Dowley

CONTENTS

The New Testament 125

Appendix

How to Use this Book

A long, long time ago, in a land very far away, a man took up a pen. He sat down and looked at a blank piece of paper. And he began to write, "In the beginning, God created the heavens and the earth." He wrote, and wrote, and wrote. His name was Moses.

Moses gave us the first five books of the Bible, from Genesis through Deuteronomy. But his books were not the only books written. It took sixty-one more books, at least thirty-six other writers, and about 1,500 years to finish the job. Only after John wrote the last word in Revelation was the Bible complete.

This makes the Bible a bit like salad – a little of this, a little of that, all mixed in together. If you have ever flipped through the pages of a Bible, you know that it is a big, complicated, unusual book. It has all kinds of writing. It has very long and very short parts. It has a lot of pages. It needs a handbook.

Bird's-eye view

This book has one purpose: to help you get a handle on the Bible. Think of being in a plane high above the ground. When you look out of the window, you can see right across the land. You are up above all the detail, where you can see the big picture. Up in the plane, you can see everything at once.

That is what this book does for you. It tells you about the big ideas in the Bible. It tells you about the main people. It gives the main points of each book in the Bible. It helps you see how all of it is put together.

Bible references

All Bible references within a chapter are from the book of the Bible covered by the chapter, unless otherwise indicated.

The Bible was originally written on papyrus scrolls.

How the Bible is Organized

The Bible has an order to it. Each book belongs in a category.
Here is how it is all organized, from beginning to end.

Minor Prophets

These books record the prophecies of God's less well-known prophets.

HOSEA
JOEL
AMOS
OBADIAH
JONAH
MICAH
NAHUM
HABAKKUK
ZEPHANIAH
HAGGAI
ZECHARIAH
MALACHI

NEW TESTAMENT

History

Four Gospels, telling the Good News about Jesus, followed by the book of Acts, which tells the story of the very first Christians.

MATTHEW
MARK
LUKE
JOHN
ACTS

ROMANS
1 CORINTHIANS
2 CORINTHIANS
GALATIANS
EPHESIANS
PHILIPPIANS
COLOSSIANS
1 THESSALONIANS
2 THESSALONIANS
1 TIMOTHY
2 TIMOTHY
TITUS
PHILEMON

Letters of Paul

These books are letters that the apostle Paul wrote.

General Letters

These books are all the New Testament letters that Paul did not write.

HEBREWS
JAMES
1 PETER
2 PETER
1 JOHN
2 JOHN
3 JOHN
JUDE

New Testament Prophecy

This book is the New Testament's only book of prophecy.

REVELATION

THE APOCRYPHA

The Apocrypha is a collection of books, and additions to Old Testament books, written between 300 BC and AD 100, sometimes also known as "deuterocanonical" books – belonging to a second "canon". Some are included in the Roman Catholic Bible, but most Protestant churches do not accept them as part of Scripture. These books include history and pious fiction.

The Old Testament

The Old Testament consists of thirty-nine books of all shapes and sizes. From the first book, Genesis, to the last book, Malachi, almost every book is different. Some books tell a story about specific people. Some give lists of rules and regulations. Some are poems. Some are sermons. God used all different kinds of people and all different kinds of writing to put together the Old Testament. He did this so that we would know how we were created. He also did this to show how he has offered his friendship to us through the many years before he came to earth as Jesus to talk with us directly.

Even though Jesus is not mentioned by name in the Old Testament, the Old Testament is in many ways about Jesus. God was teaching his people to believe that Jesus would come to earth. The Old Testament is full of sacrifices and promises of freedom. These point to what Jesus was coming to do – to offer his life as a sacrifice and set people free from sin. The Old Testament makes many prophecies, or predictions, about Jesus that came true in the New Testament.

Abram was living in Ur, in Mesopotamia, when he received a call from God to travel to the Promised Land.

In the beginning

The Old Testament starts with the story of God's creation of the world, including people, with Adam and Eve in the Garden of Eden. By the time Noah is raising his family, though, God cannot find more than a handful of righteous people on earth. After Noah is saved from the flood in a huge boat, God starts again with Noah and his three sons. From one of those sons comes Abraham. God makes a special agreement, called a covenant, with Abraham. He promises that Abraham will have a big family and that they will have a special relationship with God if they follow his laws. Abraham's family and descendants were called Hebrews, or Israelites. Today they are called the Jews.

Spotlight on the Jews

The rest of the Old Testament is about that family. The Israelites grow to be a whole nation of people. They are held captive in Egypt, but get away because of miracles that God performs through Moses. They wander through the desert back to their homeland, Israel. They win wars and lose wars. They obey God and then disobey him. The last part of the Old Testament consists of sermons by the Jewish prophets, reminding them to obey God. The prophets pointed out to them that their lives were always better when they followed God's way of doing things.

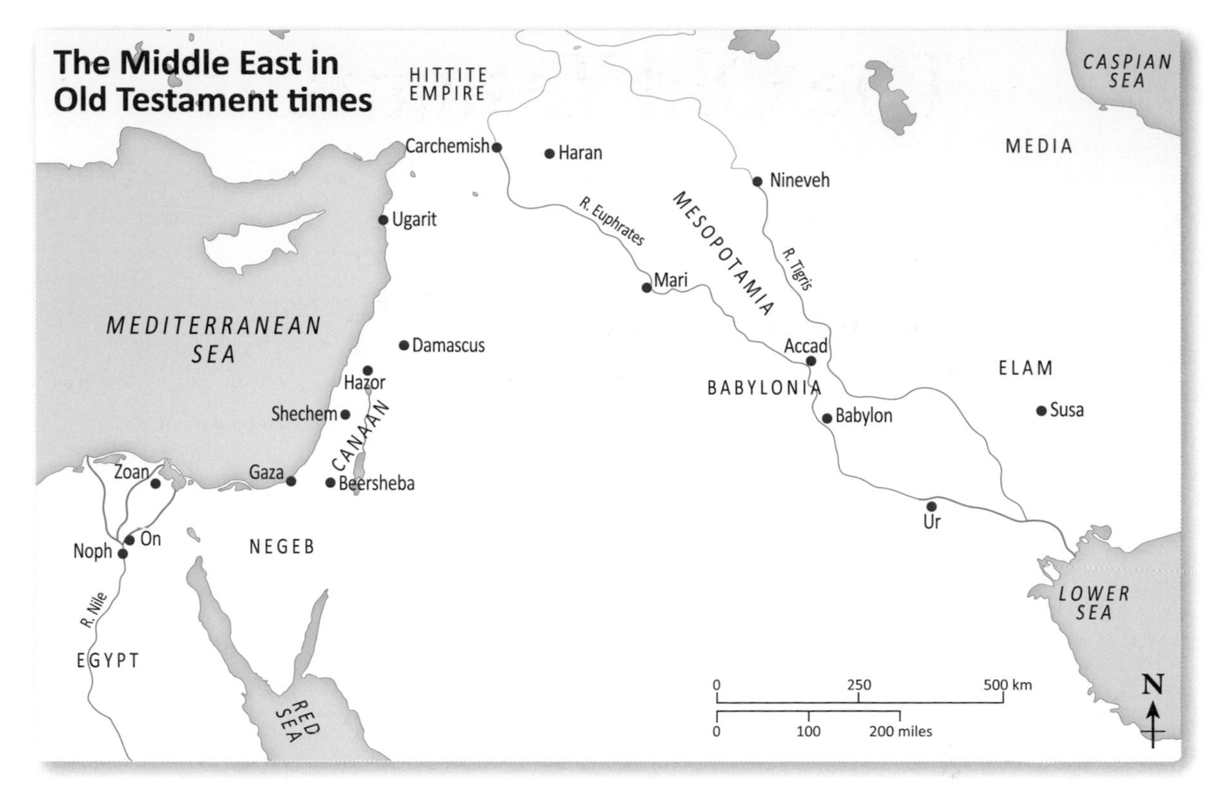

Books of the Law

The first five books of the Old Testament – Genesis, Exodus, Leviticus, Numbers, and Deuteronomy – are called the books of the Law. Genesis tells about the beginnings of the world and the beginnings of the Jewish nation. Exodus tells about the Hebrews leaving Egypt and wandering in the desert. Leviticus is a list of their rules for living. Numbers is a list of who they all were and how many were in each of the twelve "tribes", or families. Deuteronomy consists of Moses' words to his people before he died. It tells them how to follow God.

Books of history

Twelve books in the Old Testament are called history books: Joshua, Judges, Ruth, 1 and 2 Samuel, 1 and 2 Kings, 1 and 2 Chronicles, Ezra, Nehemiah, and Esther. There are other books besides these that mention facts of history, but these books specifically tell the story of Jewish history. Joshua tells of what happened to the Hebrews after Moses died. Judges tells about wise men and women that ruled Israel. Ruth tells the story of a Jewish woman who went back home to Bethlehem. 1 and 2 Samuel, 1 and 2 Kings, and 1 and 2 Chronicles tell stories of the Jewish nation and of its kings, courts, and armies. Ezra and Nehemiah tell the story of rebuilding the Temple that was planned by King David and built by King Solomon. Esther is another story about a Jewish woman who saved her people by becoming a queen.

Books of poetry

Five books are almost entirely poems or collections of poems: Job, Psalms, Proverbs, Ecclesiastes, and Song of Songs.

The Cave of Machpelah, Hebron, by tradition the resting place of the great fathers of Israel: Abraham, Isaac, and Jacob, and their wives Sarah, Rebekah, and Leah.

The words in these books don't rhyme like some poems today, but they are written in poetic language. They use word pictures and phrases to teach us about God's wisdom, strength, and love.

Books of prophecy

The last books in the Old Testament are by prophets or preachers. These prophets reminded the Jews to obey God. Five books are by major prophets: Isaiah, Jeremiah, Lamentations, Ezekiel, and Daniel. Their books and sermons are quite long and were very important to the Jewish people. There were also twelve books by minor prophets: Hosea, Joel, Amos, Obadiah, Jonah, Micah, Nahum, Habakkuk, Zephaniah, Haggai, Zechariah, and Malachi. These books are usually shorter and we know less about these writers. What we do know is that God gave them a special commission to help their people.

From the beginning to the end, the Old Testament reminds us that God is our creator, that we are to obey and worship him, and that he provides our salvation through Jesus Christ.

Old Testament Timeline

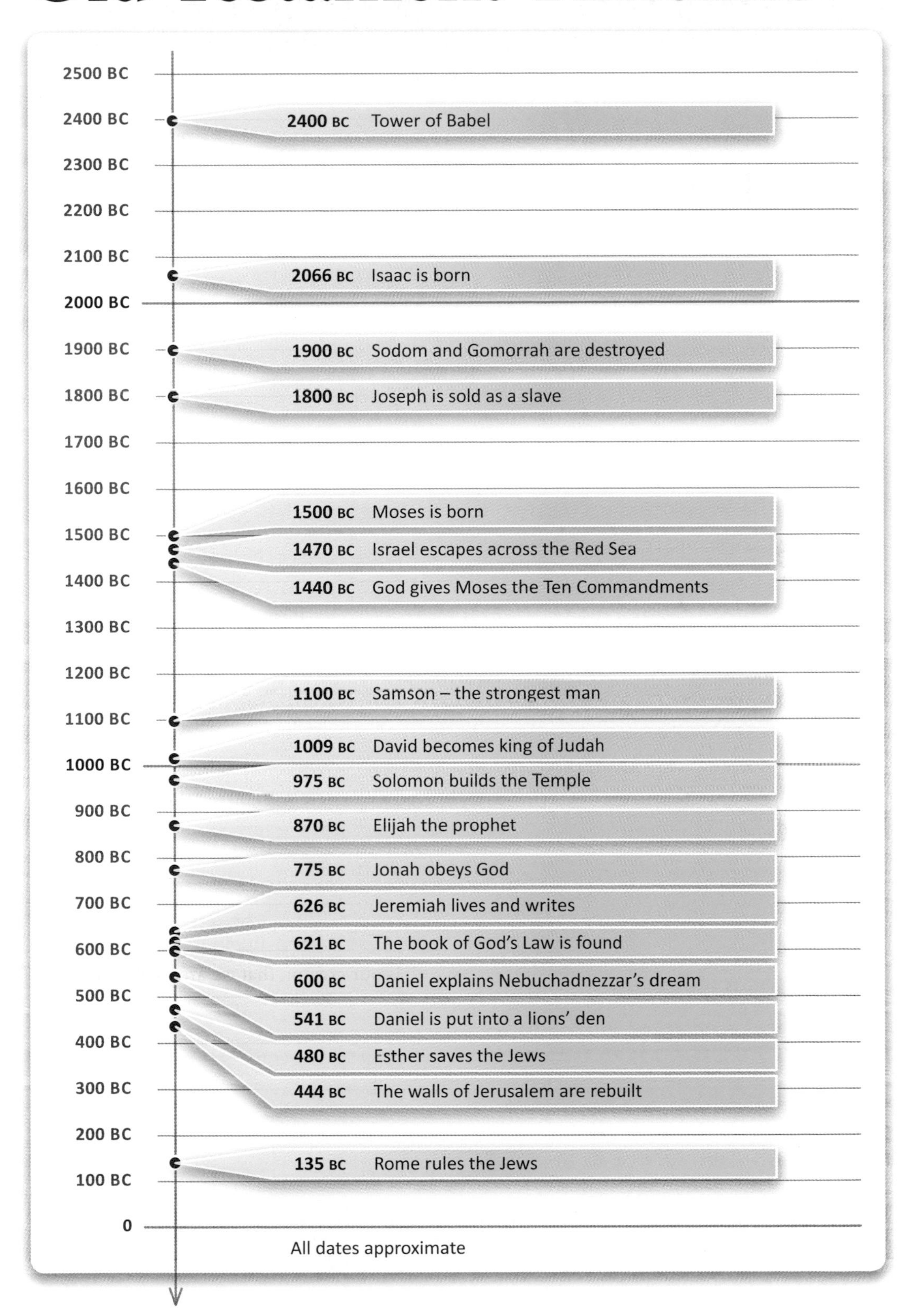

GENESIS

"In the beginning God created the heavens and the earth." (1:1)

Genesis is "the book of beginnings". It doesn't just go way back, it goes all the way back. It starts at the beginning of all beginnings. It starts at creation. It introduces us to the universe, to the earth, and to people. It introduces us to sin and to God's plans for the world. It explains what everything is and how it all got started.

Genesis also introduces us to the nation of Israel. This is very important, because in the Old Testament Israel is in the spotlight. God chose Israel to be his very own people. They play a part in each bit of God's plans to save us from sin and win us to himself. We can't understand the Bible without knowing about these people. Genesis lets us meet them for the first time.

By introducing us to all of that, Genesis introduces us to God. We learn who God is and what he really wants from us. It is amazing from start to finish.

Frequently Asked Questions

Q: Is Genesis really true?

A: Yes, we know it is true, because it is part of God's Word. Jesus quoted from Genesis a few times. He mentioned Noah, for example.

Q: Why did God ask Adam where he was and if he had eaten the forbidden fruit? Didn't God know?

A: God knows everything, but he wanted Adam to admit what he had done and repent.

Q: Why didn't Noah take more people into the ark with his family?

A: The Bible says, "Noah warned the world of God's righteous judgment" (2 Peter 2:5), but it seems people didn't believe him.

OUTLINE

Creation (1:1 – 2:3)
God creates the universe and everything in it. He makes people in his own image, like himself.

Adam and Eve (2:4 – 5:32)
Adam and Eve have all they need. But the serpent gets them to disobey God anyway. This brings sin into the world. Cain kills his brother, Abel.

Noah, the flood, and the tower of Babel (6:1 – 11:32)
The world gets so bad that God floods the whole earth. Only Noah and those on the ark with him survive.

Abraham and Sarah (12:1 – 25:18)
God chooses Abraham and Sarah to be the ancestors of his own people. God promises to bless the whole earth through this new people of God.

Isaac and Rebekah (25:19 – 28:9)
The first generation of Abraham's descendants settle in Canaan, the land God has promised them. God renews his promise to Isaac. Jacob and Rebekah trick Isaac into giving Jacob Esau's firstborn blessing.

The story of Jacob and Esau (28:10 – 36:43)
Jacob leaves home, and God promises to take care of him and bless him, just as he did Abraham and Isaac.

The story of Joseph (37:1 – 50:26)
Joseph's brothers sell him into slavery in Egypt. But God watches over him and soon Joseph is ruler of all Egypt, under Pharaoh. Through Joseph, God saves his people from famine as Jacob's entire family moves to Egypt.

The Ziggurat of Nanna at Ur. Ziggurats are huge temples found in Mesopotamia. The builders of the tower of Babel were probably attempting to build a structure of this kind.

KEY EVENTS
Abraham leaves Ur

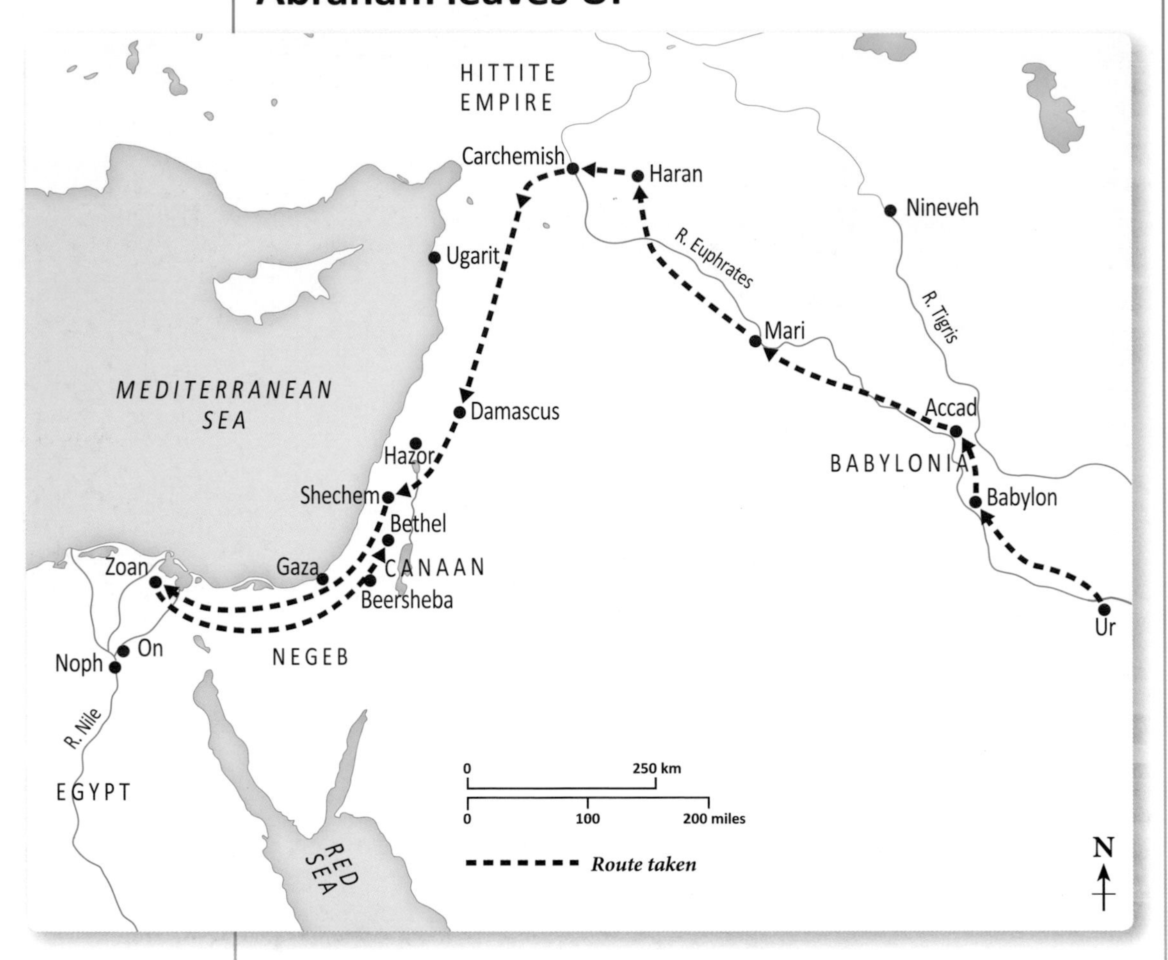

1. Ur
Ur of the Chaldeans was a thriving city with businesses and a large library. Abraham was probably well educated. When God called him to leave Ur, he had to leave all the comforts of home. (11:27–32)

2. Haran
Abraham, his father Terah, his wife Sarah, and his nephew Lot set out from Ur. They followed the Tigris and Euphrates rivers, and stopped in Haran. After Terah died, Abraham continued his journey. (12:1–5)

3. Canaan
From Haran, Abraham and his family journeyed to Shechem. God told Abraham he would give Canaan to Abraham's children. Abraham built an altar to God between Bethel and Ai, then continued to the Negeb. (12:6–9)

4. Egypt, Bethel
Because of a famine in Canaan, Abraham went to Egypt. Later he returned to Bethel with his wife and nephew. He had become very wealthy. Abraham and Lot now went separate ways: Lot chose the plain of Jordan and Abraham settled in Canaan. (12:10 – 13:18)

Jacob settles in Canaan

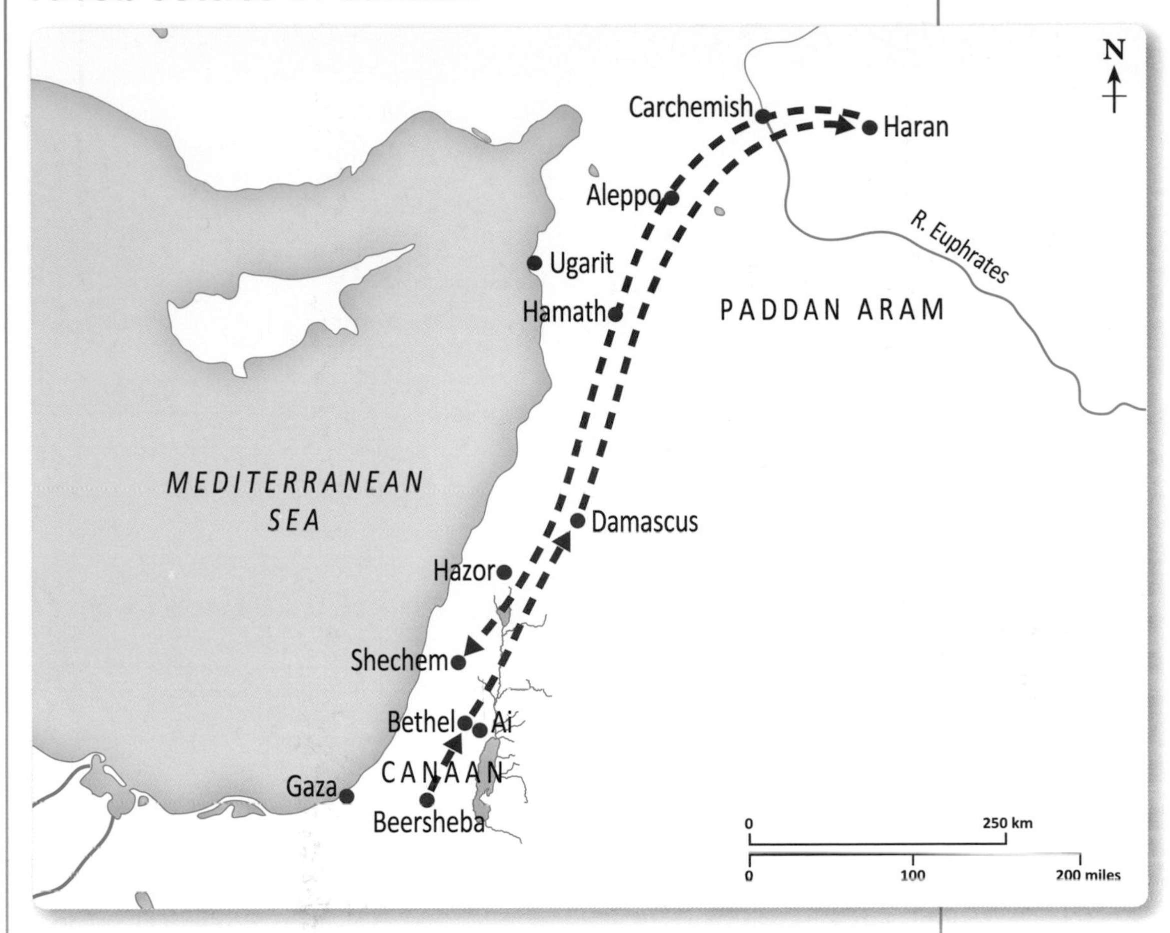

1. Beersheba

Jacob grew up in Beersheba but ran away from home after tricking his father, Isaac, and making Esau furious. (27:42–45)

2. Bethel

Jacob stopped in Bethel, where he dreamed of angels going up and down a ladder (or staircase) to heaven. God promised him Canaan for his descendants. (28:10–22)

3. Haran

In Haran, Jacob's uncle, Laban, tricked Jacob into marrying his elder daughter, Leah. Jacob worked seven extra years before he could marry Laban's younger daughter, Rachel. After twenty years' hard work, Jacob returned to Canaan. (31:36–42)

4. Canaan

Jacob was afraid of Esau, and sent gifts to him. God wrestled with Jacob and changed his name to Israel. Jacob journeyed to Shechem, where he bought a piece of property and set up an altar to worship God. (32:3 – 33:20)

Covenant

A covenant is a pact, or agreement of loyalty, between two people. Genesis records two covenants that God made with people. The first was with Noah: God promised not to destroy the earth by flood ever again (9:8–17). The rainbow became a sign of this covenant, which is still at work today.

God also made a very important covenant with Abram (Abraham). God promised to bless Abram by making him the father of a great nation (12:1–3; 15:18–21). God would give land to this nation and bless the whole world through its people. God renewed this promise to Abraham's son, Isaac (26:2–5) and to his grandson Jacob (28:13–15).

Look out for...

As you read through Genesis, look out for...

God's messages to people. *God speaks and appears to people several times at this important time in history. Notice what he says.*

Abraham. *He's a very important person in the stories of Genesis. God chooses to bless the whole world through him. Abraham's name comes up again and again in the Bible.*

Promises to Abraham. *These set the stage for a lot of what happens in the rest of the Bible.*

Joseph. *He plays a big part in his family's travels. And what Joseph does sets the stage for Exodus.*

Study Questions

- How did people become rulers of the earth? (1:26–28)
- Why did Adam and Eve have to leave the Garden of Eden? (3:22–23)
- What did God promise Noah? (8:22)
- Why did Abram leave home and go to Canaan? (12:1–3)
- Why did God allow Joseph to suffer? (50:20)

EXODUS

OUTLINE

Israel becomes a nation (1–4)

The family of Jacob (Israel) has grown to be a whole nation. Moses is born and adopted by Pharaoh's daughter. He grows up and is told by God to rescue the Hebrews from Egypt (3:1–22).

Beginning of the rescue (5–11)

Moses returns to Egypt to tell Pharaoh to free the Hebrews. God sends ten plagues to help Pharaoh make up his mind.

The Passover and Exodus (12–15)

The angel of death comes to Egypt. The Passover begins. The people leave Egypt. God parts the Red Sea.

Wilderness travels (16–19)

The Hebrews grow weary and start to complain, even though God is providing for them in every way.

Mount Sinai (20–23)

God gives Moses the Ten Commandments. God instructs his people.

The Tabernacle (24–40)

Moses meets with God. The people make a golden calf. Moses breaks the tablets of the Ten Commandments so they have to be written down again. The Tabernacle is constructed.

After 400 years in Egypt, the Hebrews were finally leaving! God knew all about their miserable lives as slaves. It was time to move out. He was taking them to the land he had promised to Abraham.

"Exodus" means "departure" or "leaving". This book tells how God freed the Hebrews from slavery in Egypt. Pharaoh didn't want to lose his slave workers. God used ten plagues to persuade Pharaoh to let the Israelites leave. Pharaoh had a hard heart! God protected his people from the plagues and also saved the Hebrews from drowning in the Red Sea.

The Hebrews had a lot to learn about being God's special people. For example, they did not always trust that God would provide food and water. They also made an idol and began to worship it. But God loved them anyway.

An Egyptian warrior.

Moses and Aaron at the court of Pharaoh. After Aaron turned his staff into a snake, Pharaoh's wise men and sorcerers did the same thing by their secret arts.

Frequently Asked Questions

Q: Why did Pharaoh like Joseph and his family but make slaves of the Israelites?
A: The pharaoh who knew Joseph was different from the pharaoh who enslaved the Israelites. 400 years had passed. During that time, the Israelites had become very numerous. This pharaoh feared they would fight him.

Q: Why did God send plagues on Egypt?
A: Egyptians had many false gods. The Lord showed his power against these false gods with each of the plagues.

Q: Why did the Israelites complain after they left Egypt?
A: The Israelites missed the Egyptian food and were afraid they couldn't get water.

Look out for...

As you read through Exodus, look out for...

Distrust. *Over and over again, the people fail to trust God, even though he takes care of them.*
Signs. *God gives the Hebrews many signs to help them believe.*
Miracles. *Throughout Exodus, God works many miracles and wonders.*

Q: What were the Israelites doing while God was giving the Ten Commandments to Moses?
A: They became impatient for Moses to return, made a golden calf as an idol, and began to worship it.

In the Desert of Sinai, Moses climbed Mount Sinai, where God gave him the Ten Commandments.

Plagues

A plague is something so bad and so big that it affects everyone around. God used ten different plagues to persuade Pharaoh to let the Israelites go. Small groups of locusts, frogs, and flies can occur in nature. But when swarms of them appear all at once, it's called a plague. Egypt had more than just a few thousand flies: there were millions of flies everywhere! God used these ten plagues to show his power to Pharaoh. Still Pharaoh did not listen. (7:14 – 12:30)

Study Questions

- What orders did Pharaoh give the Hebrew midwives? (1:15–16)
- What did the midwives do? (1:17–21)
- How did Moses' mother obey Pharaoh – but not quite? (1:22 – 2:4)
- How did God get Moses' attention? (3:1–6)
- How did blood save the Israelites? (12:21–30)
- How did God lead the Israelites out of Egypt? (13:20–22)
- In what ways did God fight the Egyptians as they chased the Israelites? (14:21–31)
- What were some of the laws that God gave the Israelites? (23:1–9)

KEY EVENTS

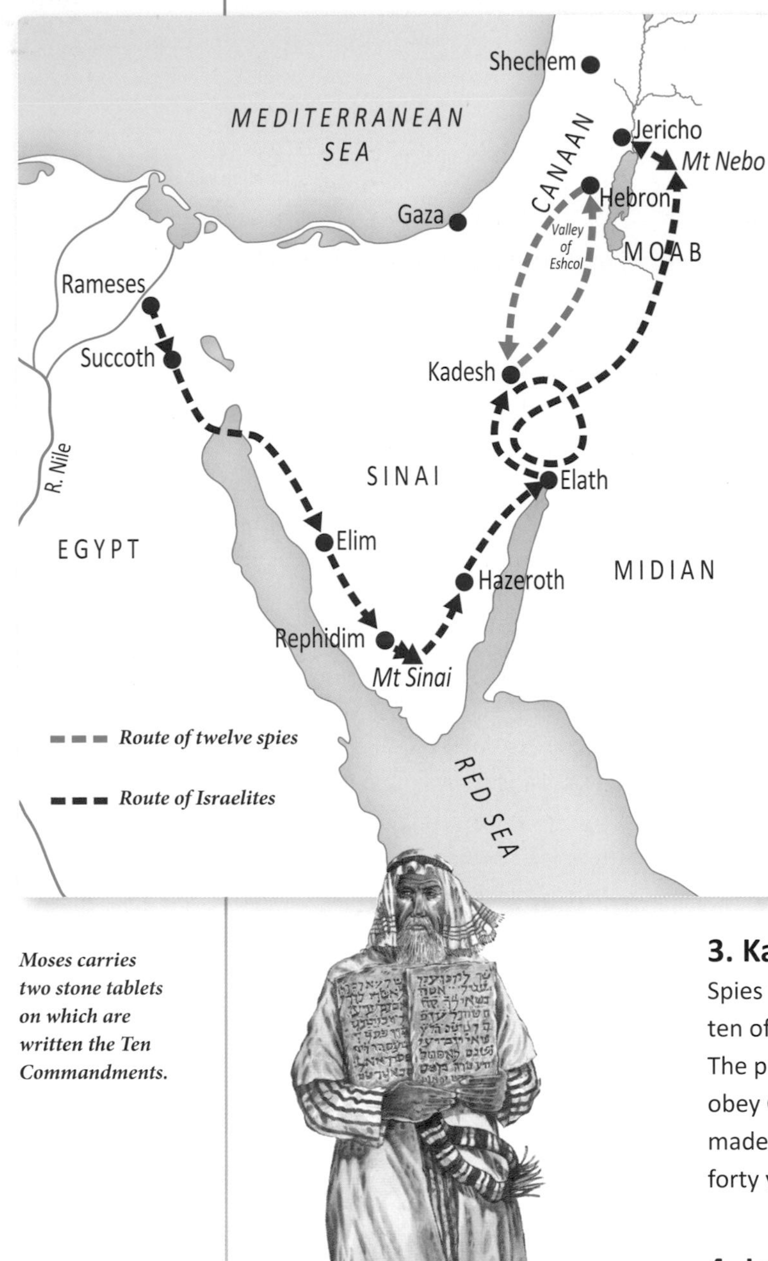

Moses carries two stone tablets on which are written the Ten Commandments.

The Exodus

1. Elim and Rephidim

Moses crossed the Red Sea, then led his people south. The desert was hot and dry, but God provided water and food, and helped the Israelites defeat their enemy, the Amalekites. (14:21–25; 16:1, 13–15; 17:1–15)

2. Mount Sinai

For almost a year, the Israelites camped at the foot of Mount Sinai. God gave them the Ten Commandments and the plan for the Tabernacle. (19–40)

3. Kadesh

Spies went into the Promised Land, but ten of the twelve gave a bad report. The people were scared and wouldn't obey God's command to enter. God made them wander in the desert for forty years. (Numbers 13–14)

4. Jericho

Moses died on Mount Nebo. Joshua led the people across the Jordan River on dry land, defeated Jericho and began to take Canaan. (Joshua 1–6)

LEVITICUS

OUTLINE

The system of sacrifices and the priests (1–10)

Notes on how to offer sacrifices. The priests begin their work.

Laws of sanitation and health (11–15)

Notes on how to keep themselves and their camp clean.

The annual atonement (16–17)

Notes on how to celebrate the yearly Day of Atonement.

Holy living (18–22)

Notes on actions that God hates. Also many laws and rules.

The priests, their services, and their duties (23–24)

Notes on the festivals and special days, called holy days (like our "holidays") and the role of the priests in the celebrations.

Special years; warnings and blessings; vows and tithes (25–27)

Notes on traditions the people should keep, such as the sabbath year and the year of jubilee. Also a pledge that there will be blessings for obedience and punishments for disobedience.

Making the Israelites into a special nation took a lot of work. God had to teach his people a whole new way of life. So in the book of Leviticus he gave them a lot of instructions on how to live and how to worship.

Leviticus was a handbook for the Hebrew priests. It taught about the sacrifices God wanted people to offer for forgiveness. It was also a guide for holy living. Leviticus mentions holiness lots of times. A special verse says, "You must be holy because I, the Lord your God, am holy" (19:2).

God gave clear directions for worship. Two of Aaron's sons disobeyed these rules. It was such a serious matter that they died. The offerings described in Leviticus help us understand why Jesus came and died.

The high priest wore a breastplate with twelve precious stones. Each stone represented one of the tribes of Israel.

Priests make a burnt offering on the great altar that stood in front of the Israelite Tabernacle. The priest in the foreground is blowing a shofar, a ram's-horn trumpet.

Passover lamb

In the final plague on Egypt, the oldest son of every household died unless lamb's blood was smeared on the frame of the door of the house. The Israelites smeared their doorposts, and the angel of death "passed over". From then on, they celebrated this "Passover" with a special meal each year at the same time (23:2, 4–5).

This meal reminded them of God's rescue. But it also teaches us about the work Jesus would do. When Jesus died on the cross, he became our Passover lamb and saved us from death (John 1:29, 36).

Frequently Asked Questions

Q: Why did the people have to sacrifice animals?

A: God wanted the people to understand how serious sin is.

Q: What kind of animals did God want as offerings?

A: The offerings God wanted were bulls, lambs, goats, doves, and pigeons, depending on the occasion. But the offering always had to be a perfect animal. It had to be the best – not an animal with a blemish or a disease.

Q: Why did the people have to keep on offering sacrifices?

A: These sacrifices did not really take away sin, but made amends for offending against God. People sin again and again, so before Jesus came, people had to offer sacrifices again and again. But Jesus' death on the cross took away sin; his sacrifice for sin was needed only once.

The shofar *is still used today in Jewish worship. It announces the start of the solemn Day of Atonement,* Yom Kippur.

Look out for…

As you read through Leviticus, look out for…

Holiness. *This whole book is about holiness. Over and over again, God teaches his people to be holy.*

Priests. *This book is like a manual for priests. Because of this, you will find lots of references to priests.*

Sacrifices. *Sacrifices were to be an important part of Jewish worship. The first part of Leviticus tells how these sacrifices were to be done.*

Festivals and holy days. *God uses the Jewish festivals and holy days to remind the people of the miracles he has performed among them, just as Christmas reminds us of Jesus' birth.*

Study Questions

- How did Aaron and the priests know God cared about holiness? (10:1–11)
- What rewards did God promise the Israelites if they obeyed him? (26:1–13)
- What did God say to the people who did not want to obey him? (26:14–17)
- How do we know the book of Leviticus is important? (27:34)

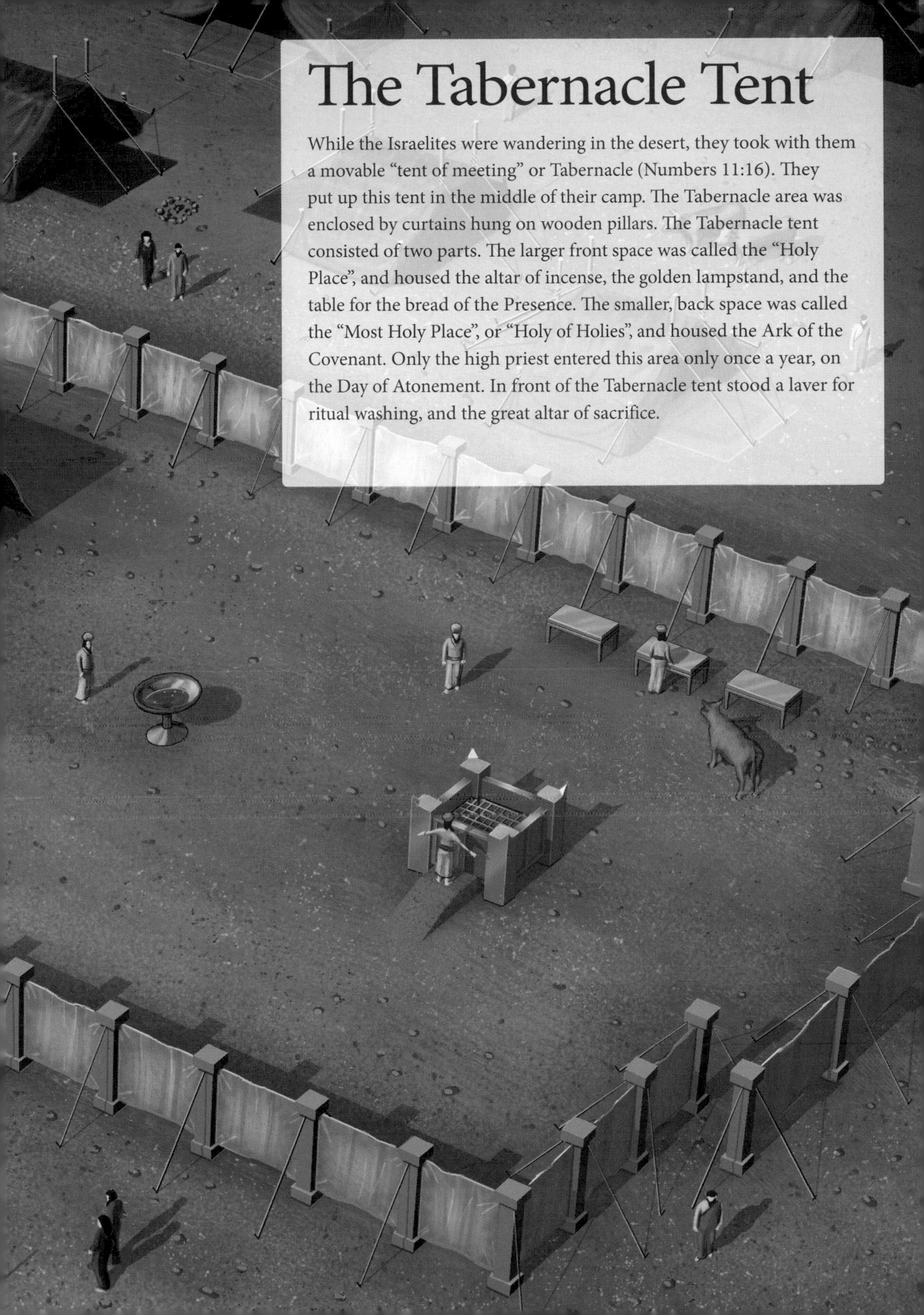

The Tabernacle Tent

While the Israelites were wandering in the desert, they took with them a movable "tent of meeting" or Tabernacle (Numbers 11:16). They put up this tent in the middle of their camp. The Tabernacle area was enclosed by curtains hung on wooden pillars. The Tabernacle tent consisted of two parts. The larger front space was called the "Holy Place", and housed the altar of incense, the golden lampstand, and the table for the bread of the Presence. The smaller, back space was called the "Most Holy Place", or "Holy of Holies", and housed the Ark of the Covenant. Only the high priest entered this area only once a year, on the Day of Atonement. In front of the Tabernacle tent stood a laver for ritual washing, and the great altar of sacrifice.

Numbers

After all that God did in Egypt to prove he was God, the people of Israel still doubted him. The book of Numbers tells about the test of faith they faced.

The book gets its name from the fact that the people of Israel were numbered, or counted, twice. The first time they were counted was soon after they had left Egypt. God wanted Moses to know how many fighting men he had. But the people grumbled and complained and didn't believe God could take them into the Promised Land.

Moses sent twelve spies to see how best they should conquer that land. When they returned, ten said it was impossible. Only two – Joshua and Caleb – said, yes, there were giants, yes, it was a big job, but yes, the Lord would give them the victory as he had said. But the people listened to the ten frightened men. They refused to go into battle!

Because they doubted, they spent forty years wandering in the desert. None of the people who doubted God lived to see his promise fulfilled.

At the end of this long, winding trip, Moses counted the people again.

"The Lord said to Moses, 'Choose a leader from each tribe and send them into Canaan to explore the land I am giving you.'" (13:1–2, CEV)

OUTLINE

Numbering and organizing the people (1–5)
Moses and Aaron count the people of Israel for the first time and begin to give certain jobs to certain tribes.

Preparing for the journey (6–10)
The people get ready to travel by offering sacrifices and celebrating their first Passover in freedom.

Marching to Kadesh (11–12)
The people complain because the trip is so difficult. Some even wish they were back in Egypt. God provides for them by sending quail to eat.

God sent the people quail to eat.

The twelve spies (13–14)
Spies explore the land. Only two bring back a good report. The other ten are afraid the Israelites will never be able to conquer the land. The people become afraid and disturbed. Once again, they don't trust God.

More lack of faith (15–21)
The people rebel against Moses. God uses an earthquake to punish them. Aaron's family begin to act as priests when a walking stick starts to bud as if it were a living plant.

Balaam's prophecy and a problem with the kingdom of Moab (22–25)
Balaam comes to curse Israel, but blesses it instead. His own donkey talks to him. Then the Israelites get tricked by people who worship idols.

Another count, a new ruler, more rules (26–36)
The people of Israel are counted a second time. Joshua becomes the next leader of the Israelites. Two tribes receive their portion of land, because they want to settle before crossing the River Jordan.

During their long years in the desert, the Israelites lived in tents.

Frequently Asked Questions

Q: Why were the people counted?
A: Men who were twenty years or older were counted so they could serve in the army.

Q: As there were no phones, how did Moses tell the people they were to move on?
A: God told Moses to make two silver trumpets to call the people together and move camp.

Q: Why were Miriam and Aaron jealous of their brother, Moses?
A: They too wanted to be important leaders.

Q: Why didn't ten of the spies want to enter Canaan?
A: The spies thought the people of Canaan were so large that they felt like grasshoppers and were afraid.

Look out for...

As you read through Numbers, look out for...

Rules and regulations. *Numbers gives many guidelines – especially for priests – on how to do things.*

Lack of faith. *The people of God keep losing their faith even though God has provided for them.*

Counting. *The whole Hebrew nation is counted twice. They have no computers, so this is a big job.*

Study Questions

- How did God guide the people from place to place? (9:15–23)
- What was manna like? (11:7–9)
- Why did Moses lose the chance to enter the Promised Land? (20:2–12)
- How did Balaam's donkey make Balaam look silly when he tried to curse God's people? (22:21–33)
- Before he died, what did Moses ask God to do? (27:12–23)
- What was a city of refuge? (35:9–15)

Deuteronomy

OUTLINE

Story of the journey (1–5)

The Hebrews leave Mount Sinai, where they received the Ten Commandments. Moses appoints leaders for each tribe. The people wander through the desert and fight battles.

Rules and regulations (5–26)

Moses reviews the Ten Commandments and many other rules for living.

Curses and blessings (27–30)

Moses reminds the people that they will receive blessings for obedience and curses for disobedience.

Moses' successor (31–34)

Joshua becomes the leader of the Israelites and Moses says goodbye to his people. Moses dies in the land of Moab and never enters the Promised Land.

Deuteronomy is a book of memories, like a scrapbook. Moses had spent forty years taking the Israelites on a journey that was supposed to have taken only two years. The people who disobeyed God all died without seeing the Promised Land. But now the people who came after them were about to enter Canaan.

Moses reminded them of all that God had done for them over the past forty years. He repeated the Law. He told them to believe God and do God's will.

Moses reminded the people of God's promises for obedience and the punishment for disobedience. He also blessed the people. Then Moses made Joshua their new leader.

Deuteronomy is the fifth book of the Law. Jesus knew it well. It is the book Jesus quoted when Satan tried to tempt him to disobey his Father.

The bare slopes of Mount Sinai, where Moses received the Ten Commandments.

A Jewish family remembers the deliverance from Egypt in the annual festival of Passover.

A special Seder plate and cup, used at Passover.

Look out for...

As you read through Deuteronomy, look out for...

The Ten Commandments. *This book retells some of the stories from Exodus, including how God gave Moses the Ten Commandments.*

God's faithfulness. *Even when the Hebrews do not have much faith, God faithfully takes care of them.*

What God requires. *God tells the people clearly what he wants: their worship, love, and obedience.*

Celebrations. *God does not just give his people rules; he also tells them to hold festivals to remind them of the good things God has done.*

Frequently Asked Questions

Q: Why wasn't Moses allowed to enter the Promised Land?

A: Moses had disobeyed God. He had been angry with the people for complaining. Instead of asking the rock for water, as God had told him to, Moses had hit the rock.

Q: Why was Moses afraid the people would forget God?

A: Moses knew that when the people had plenty of food and an easy life they might forget to trust God.

Q: How did God take care of his people in the desert?

A: God sent bread from heaven called "manna" and water for them to drink. Also, their sandals did not wear out for forty years!

The view from Mount Nebo, Jordan.

The Promised Land

Many years before the Exodus from Egypt, God had promised Abraham some land. We know that land today as Israel. You may hear of people going to "the Holy Land". They mean the land where Jesus grew up. It is the same land that God promised Abraham and that the Hebrews journeyed to from Egypt.

Moses looked into the Promised Land from Mount Nebo.

Deuteronomy describes the time just before the nation first entered the Promised Land. In this book, they are just across the river from this land. Moses goes to the top of the mountain to look across and see the land that is theirs. This land has always been, and always will be, important to the Jewish people. (1:6–8)

Study Questions

- What are the Ten Commandments? (5:6–21)
- What is one reason that God wants people to obey him with all their heart? (5:29)
- How did God say parents should teach their children God's laws? (6:6–9)
- Before Moses died, what was so important about the advice he gave Joshua? (31:7–8)
- What was Moses like at the end of his life? (34:7)
- How was Moses special? (34:10–12)

JOSHUA

The Israelites cross the River Jordan and finally enter the Promised Land. The priests carry the Ark of the Covenant on their shoulders.

The Israelites needed a strong leader to take them into the Promised Land. Joshua took up where Moses left off. Finally, the people were ready to follow God's plan. It may have seemed a strange plan, but it worked. The book of Joshua tells about the battles the Israelites had in taking the land that God had given them.

God dried up the waters of the River Jordan so the Israelites could cross over on dry land. Marching around a city doesn't sound like the way to win a battle. But the Israelites obeyed God. Once each day for six days they marched around Jericho. On the seventh day, they marched around seven times. The seventh time, Joshua told the people to shout. They shouted and the walls of Jericho came crashing down.

This was just the beginning of conquering the land God had promised to Abraham, Isaac, and Jacob. Sometimes the people disobeyed, and then they failed. But God took them into Canaan and gave each tribe a new home.

Joshua's instructions to the people are also found in this book. Like Moses, Joshua wanted his people to obey God and enjoy God's blessings.

Archaeologists have discovered many ancient remains at the site of the city of Jericho.

OUTLINE

Joshua becomes leader (1)

God tells Joshua how to be successful. Joshua takes charge of the people and begins to lead.

Taking over Canaan (2–12)

Some spies go to Jericho and are taken care of by a woman named Rahab. God parts the River Jordan for all the people to cross. The people circle Jericho and the walls fall down. Rahab and her family are spared. Achan gets greedy and everyone suffers for it.

Dividing and settling the land (13–22)

The people occupy the land and continue to fight the few people who will not let them settle in peace.

Joshua says goodbye (23–24)

Joshua gives a final, inspiring speech. He reminds the people of everything God has done for them.

Frequently Asked Questions

Q: What made Joshua brave enough to take Moses' place?

A: God told Joshua he would be with him wherever he went.

Q: Why did Rahab hide the Israelite spies from her own people?

A: Rahab had heard about God's power, and decided to follow him instead of her people's false gods.

Q: How did the Israelites know which people were on their side?

A: Rahab put a red cord in the window of her house. Everyone inside the house was saved.

Q: How did the Israelites defeat great Jericho easily, but were themselves defeated by the little town of Ai?

A: Achan had hidden some treasures in his tent, against God's instructions. All the Israelites suffered for his selfishness by losing the battle against Ai.

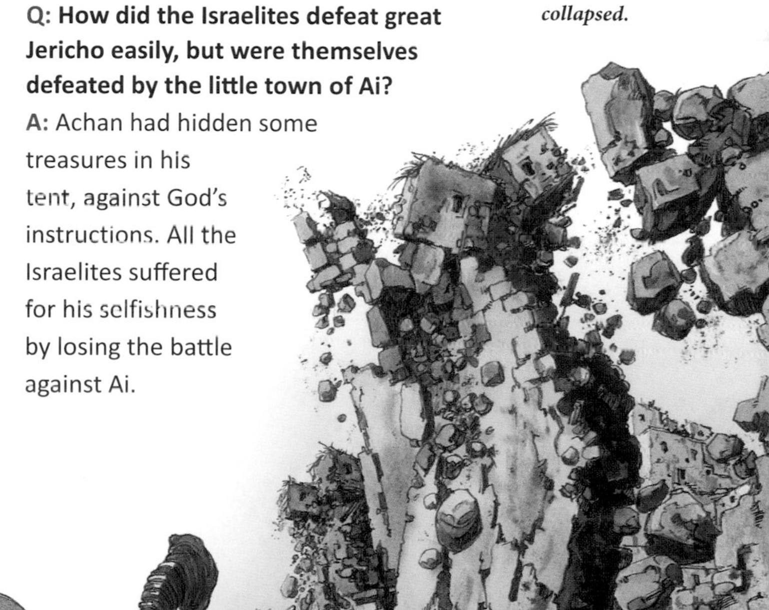

On the seventh day of marching around Jericho, the priests blew their trumpets, the Israelites shouted, and the great walls collapsed.

Tribes

After the land had been captured, it was divided between "tribes". Tribes are large family units – not just parents and children, but all their distant relatives too. A tribe starts way back with the parents' parents and the grandparents' parents. A tribe traces its roots right back to one person.

The tribes of Israel come from ten of Jacob's sons and two of his grandsons. (Jacob was Abraham's grandson. God promised Abraham that his descendants would be as many as the stars in the sky.) Whenever the book of Joshua talks about a tribe, it means the families that came from one of those sons. Every tribe got some land, except the tribe of Levi. Levi is the tribe that Moses and his family came from. This tribe became priests, leaders of worship, and caretakers of the Temple. Because they worked in the Temple, they did not need land.

The twelve tribes

Reuben	Asher
Simeon	Issachar
Judah	Zebulun
Dan	Benjamin
Naphtali	Manasseh*
Gad	Ephraim*

*Manasseh and Ephraim were sons of Joseph.

Look out for...

As you read through Joshua, look out for...

Battles. *There are many important and miraculous battles.*

Good leadership. *Joshua is a strong leader who takes good care of God's people.*

Wins and losses. *When the people obey and trust God, the battles go well. But when they do not... watch what happens!*

Miracles. *God keeps doing miracles for his people. The sun stands still, the waters part, and many other miracles take place.*

Study Questions

- What made Rahab want to help the Israelite spies? (2:8–13)
- Why did Joshua set up twelve stones at Gilgal? (4:19–24)
- How did Joshua make sure the people knew what God expected and what he promised? (8:30–35)
- How did the people of Gibeon trick Joshua? (9:1–27)
- How did Joshua gain extra daylight hours to win a battle? (10:9–14)
- How did God keep his promises to the Israelites? (21:43–45)

KEY EVENTS
The conquest of Canaan

1. River Jordan
The priests carried the Ark of the Covenant into the River Jordan. The water stopped flowing and everyone crossed over on dry ground (2:1 – 4:24). Once in the Promised Land, they camped at Gilgal and celebrated Passover. (5:13 – 6:5)

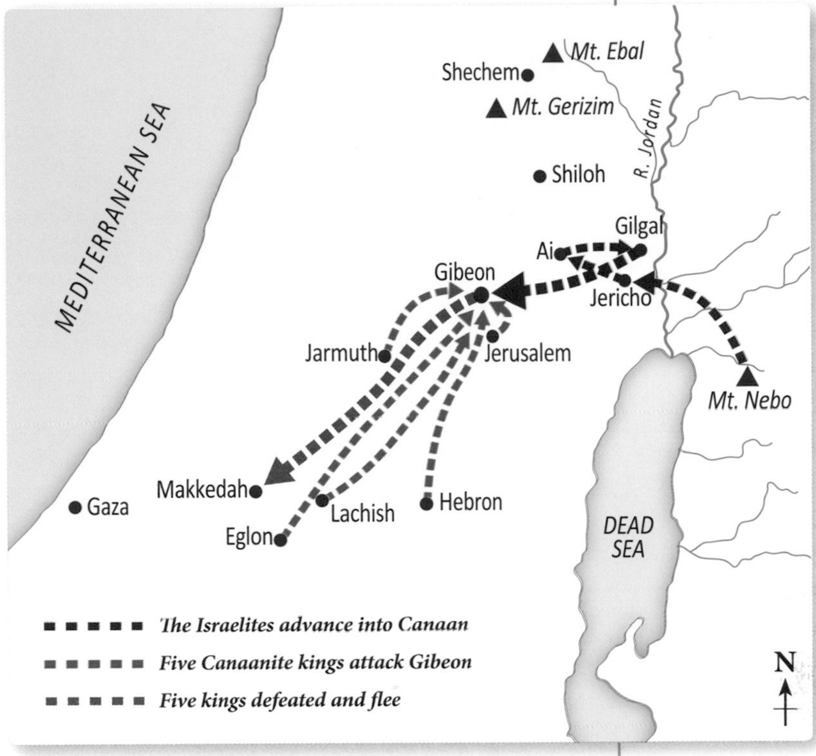

2. Jericho and Ai
Joshua and the people obeyed God and broke the walls of Jericho down by marching around the city (6:1–27). Because of Achan's sin, the Israelites were unable to take the next city, Ai. But after dealing with Achan, they captured Ai. (7:1 – 8:29)

3. Mount Ebal and Mount Gerizim
Joshua, the priests, and the people renewed their covenant with God. (8:30–35)

4. Gibeon
Five kings attacked the city of Gibeon, which had made a treaty with the Israelites. Joshua and his troops joined the battle. It lasted all day, and Joshua asked God to make the sun stand still until the Israelites defeated the enemy. (10:1–43)

5. Hazor
Another group of kings joined together to fight Israel. But God gave his people the victory. (11:1–23)

6. Shiloh
Many of the enemy armies were defeated and the Israelites enjoyed a time of peace. They gathered in Shiloh and set up the Tabernacle to worship God. (18:1 – 19:51)

JUDGES

Gideon defeats the Midianites with a tiny force of 300 men, equipped with burning torches and trumpets. (Chapter 7)

The great leaders Moses and Joshua were dead. The Israelites had seen God keep his promise to take them into the Promised Land. But they became lazy about obeying God. They didn't remove the sinful people who lived in Canaan. Instead, the Israelites copied the ways of their enemies. The book of Judges tells of the trouble and sorrow the Israelites went through.

The people of Israel married people who had idols as gods. Soon the Israelites themselves turned to these false gods. God punished them for turning their backs on him. Instead of enjoying the good things of the Promised Land, the Israelites suffered war, slavery, and hardship. But when they cried to God for help, he sent a judge to lead them into battle and bring them back to himself.

Again and again, the Israelites forgot their promise to obey God. So, again and again, he allowed their enemies to defeat them. Then the Israelites would be sorry for their sins and ask him to save them, and God would send another judge to help them.

For about 325 years, this pattern continued. God used thirteen men and women to judge and help his people. The judges were not perfect, but they followed God's leadership. And he used them to help his people.

OUTLINE

Introduction (1–2)

The Hebrews do not conquer all of the Promised Land. This means some of their enemies are left to cause trouble. It's these enemies that the judges have to fight.

Israel's first judges (3)

Othniel, Ehud, and Shamgar serve as Israel's judges.

Sisera is defeated (4–5)

Deborah defends Israel with Barak's help, and defeats Sisera.

Gideon defends Israel (6–10)

Gideon, Abimelech, Tola, and Jair serve as judges. Gideon defeats the Midianites with a tiny army.

Jephthah defends Israel (11–12)

Jephthah, Ibzan, Elon, and Abdon serve as judges.

Samson (13–16)

God makes Samson especially strong to defend Israel, but he is betrayed by Delilah.

Israel without a leader (17–21)

This is a time of much confusion in the life of God's people.

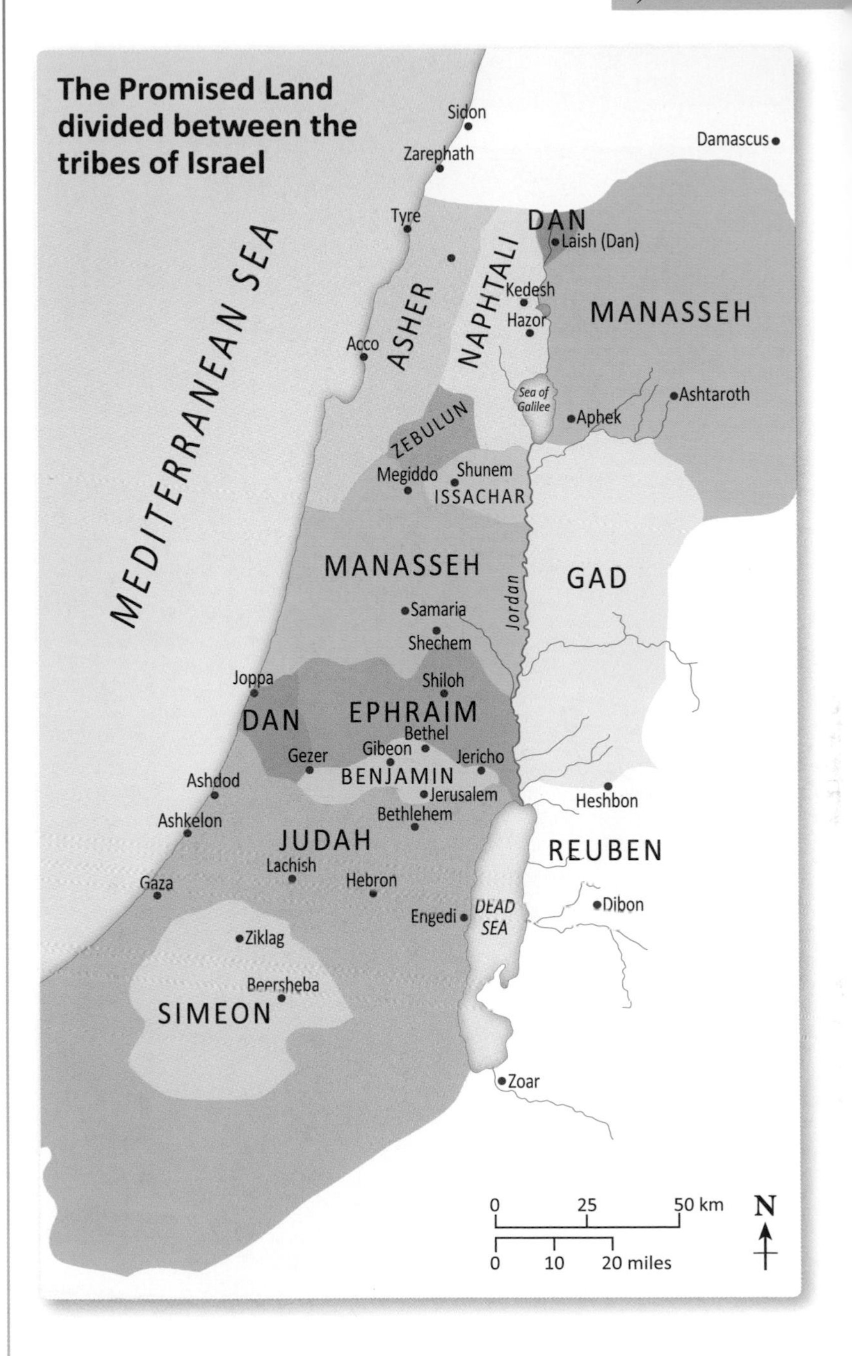

Samson and Delilah. Samson once killed a thousand Philistines with a donkey's jawbone.

Nazirites

Nazirites were people who kept strict religious laws. A person could be a Nazirite for his or her whole life, or for just a short time. Nazirites did not drink wine or eat grapes. This showed they were willing to give up something enjoyable to serve God. Also, they never cut their hair or used a razor. Three well-known characters from the Bible were Nazirites for life: Samson, Samuel, and John the Baptist. (Judges 13; 1 Samuel 1; Luke 1:11–17)

Study Questions

- Why did Othniel become the first judge of Israel? (3:7–11)
- What went wrong with Israel during the time of the judges? (21:25)

Look out for...

As you read through Judges, look out for...

Falling away. *Israel goes through patterns of following God, then falling away from him.*

Revival. *Good strong judges help bring Israel back to God.*

Rebellion. *Whenever the Israelites turn away from God, they lead evil, violent lives.*

Frequently Asked Questions

Q: Why didn't God keep his promise to help his people?
A: God promised to bless the Israelites if they obeyed him. When they disobeyed, he stopped helping them. But he still sent judges who were able to defend Israel from its enemies.

Q: Who were judges?
A: Judges were leaders God called to help the Israelites. They showed the people their wrongdoing, encouraged them, led them in battle, and brought them back to God. Sometimes they ruled foolishly.

Q: Who were the greatest judges?
A: Most people think Gideon, Deborah, and Samson were the greatest judges.

RUTH

It was a dark time in the history of the Israelites. Everyone was doing what he or she wanted. Very few people were trying to obey God. Few people thought of helping others. In this unhappy time were three people whose lives were different; their story is told in the book of Ruth.

Naomi, Ruth, and Boaz did not just think of themselves. They thought about what would be good for others and helped those in need. They also loved God.

Ruth was a widow (her husband had died). She lived in the land of Moab with her mother-in-law, Naomi. Naomi was a widow too. Naomi wanted to return to Bethlehem in Judah. She told Ruth to stay in Moab and go back to her people. But Ruth loved her mother-in-law.

Ruth promised to go with Naomi and take care of her. She also wanted to worship the true God.

When Naomi and Ruth arrived in Bethlehem, Ruth worked to get food for them. Boaz was kind and told Ruth she could collect grain in his fields. In the end, Boaz married Ruth. Then he and Ruth took care of Naomi together.

The book of Ruth shows that no matter how bad things are, there are always some people who love God.

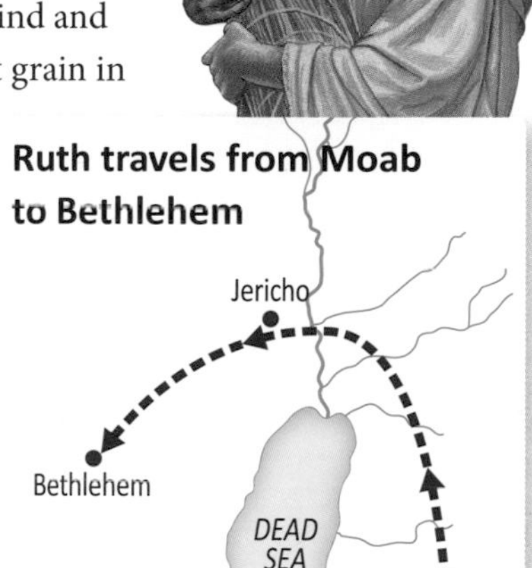

OUTLINE

Naomi in Moab (1)

Naomi's husband and sons die, and she decides to move back to Bethlehem. One of her daughters-in-law, Ruth, goes with her.

Ruth meets Boaz (2)

Ruth gathers wheat in a field owned by Boaz. Boaz is nearly Naomi's closest relative in town.

Ruth asks Boaz to take care of her (3)

According to Jewish law, a relative such as Boaz could marry Ruth and take care of her. Ruth asks him to do so.

Boaz marries Ruth (4)

Ruth and Boaz marry and have children.

The rich farmer Boaz saw poor Ruth gathering leftover grain in his field.

Look out for...

As you read through Ruth, look out for...

Loyalty. *Ruth shows loyalty to Naomi by leaving her own homeland to be with Naomi.*

Relationships. *This story is all about relationships between Naomi and Ruth; Ruth and Boaz; and Ruth, Boaz, and their son.*

Courage. *Ruth, Naomi, and Boaz all show courage.*

Ruth and Boaz married and had a son. David was among their descendants.

Frequently Asked Questions

Q: Why were Naomi and her family in Moab?

A: There had been a famine in Judah. Naomi, her husband, and her two sons went to Moab to find food.

Q: Why did Naomi need Ruth to take care of her?

A: In her day, widows were treated badly or ignored. They became poor and had little unless a family member helped them.

Study Questions

- Why did Naomi agree to let Ruth go with her to Bethlehem? (1:15–18)
- What did Boaz hear about Ruth? (2:11–12)
- What kind of man was Boaz? (2:19–20)
- How did God bless Ruth, Boaz, and Naomi? (4:13–17)

1 SAMUEL

The book of 1 Samuel is named after the man who was last, first, and best – all rolled into one. Samuel was the last judge of Israel. He was the first prophet after Moses. He was also one of the best prophets of Israel. On top of all that, Samuel was a priest.

During Samuel's leadership, the people of Israel decided they didn't want a spiritual leader; like all the nations around them, they wanted a king. Samuel tried to tell them of the problems and trouble they would have if they got a king. But the people would not listen. They wanted a king anyway. So although it was not his first choice for them, God let the people have a king.

Saul became the first king of the Israelites. Samuel was the priest who anointed him. In Old Testament times, when a king was appointed, it was the custom for a priest to pour oil on his head. This "anointing" was a sign that God had chosen him, and that God had poured his spirit on him.

This history book of Israel records Saul's good start, his disobedience to God, and his final failure. Other important stories of Israel in 1 Samuel are David and Goliath, David's friendship with Jonathan, Saul's attempts to kill David, and the death of Saul.

Samuel visited Jesse to find a king to succeed Saul. God showed him that of all Jesse's sons, David, the young shepherd boy, was the chosen one. Samuel is depicted anointing David.

Saul's royal palace was at Gibeah, just north of Jerusalem.

OUTLINE

Samuel as a child and a judge (1–8)

Hannah prays for a child and God gives her Samuel. Samuel grows up in the Temple and becomes a great prophet. The Israelites ask for a king, and Samuel warns them of the dangers in following a man instead of God.

Saul's rise to power (9–14)

Samuel anoints Saul as Israel's first king. Saul wins some victories but also makes mistakes.

Saul's decline and his struggles with David (15–31)

Saul begins to fail as a leader. Samuel anoints David as future king. David kills Goliath. At first, Saul and David are friends, and Saul's son Jonathan is David's best friend. Then Saul becomes jealous of David, because the people speak of David as a great leader. By the time of Saul's death, Saul sees David as an enemy.

Frequently Asked Questions

Q: How could Samuel have so many important jobs?

A: Samuel's mother, Hannah, asked God for a son. She promised to give him back to God to serve him. Since he was a child, Samuel was training to serve God. God was able to use him in many ways.

Q: Why did the Israelites want a king?

A: Samuel was getting old, and his sons did not follow his good example. They were very bad leaders. The people used this as an excuse to have a king.

Q: What kind of man was Saul?

A: Saul was tall and handsome, the son of a wealthy man. He was humble at first, but later became proud and jealous of David. He also began to pick and choose when he would obey God.

KEY EVENTS
The formation of the kingdom of Israel

1. Ramah

Saul was looking for his father's lost donkeys. He didn't know the prophet Samuel was waiting for him at his home in Ramah. The people wanted a king, and God told Samuel to anoint Saul as king of Israel. (7:15–17; 9:3 – 10:1)

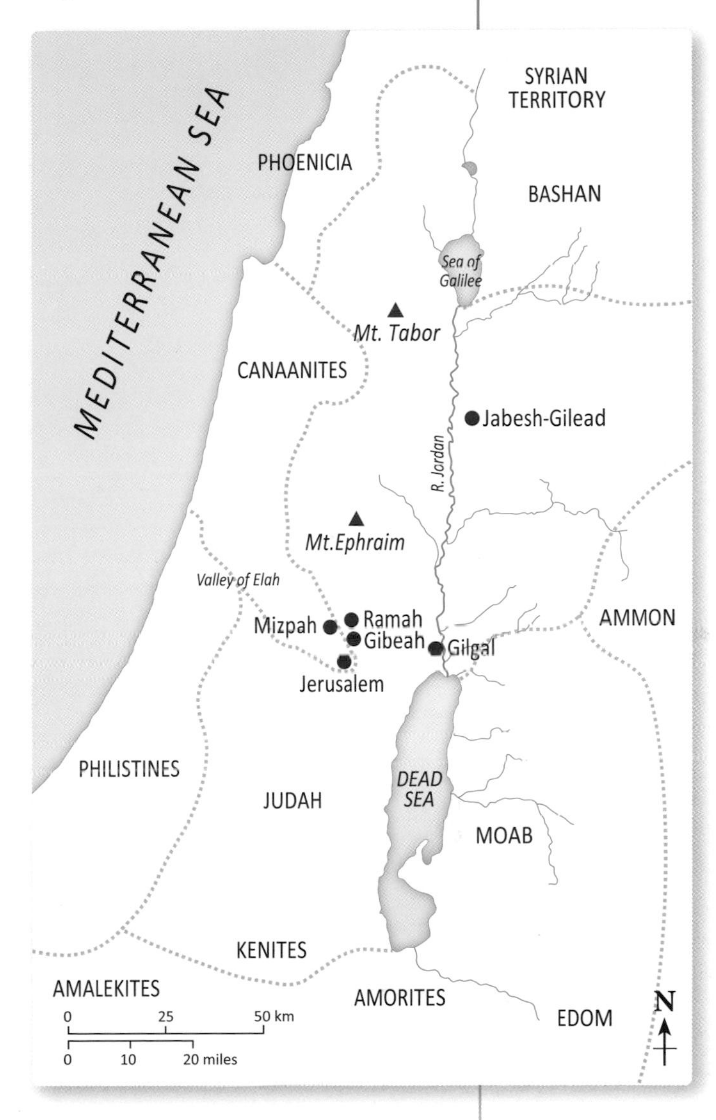

2. Jabesh Gilead

The people of Jabesh Gilead were besieged and asked Saul for help. Saul gathered an army and rescued them. The people celebrated by going to Gilgal to worship God and confirmed Saul as their new king. (11:1–15)

3. Elah

Saul gathered his army in the valley of Elah to fight the Philistines. The giant Goliath mocked them and challenged any one Israelite to a fight. David accepted the challenge and killed Goliath with his shepherd's sling and a stone. The Philistines fled, but were pursued by the Israelites. From then on, David helped Saul to defeat their enemies and became very popular. (17:1 – 18:5)

4. Hebron

King Saul was jealous of David because the people loved him. For years, Saul chased David and tried to kill him. Then Saul was killed in battle by the Philistines. The people of Hebron made David king of Judah. (2 Samuel 2:4)

5. Jerusalem

Seven and a half years after Saul's death, David became king over all the tribes of Israel and made Jerusalem his capital. (2 Samuel 5:4–7)

Philistines

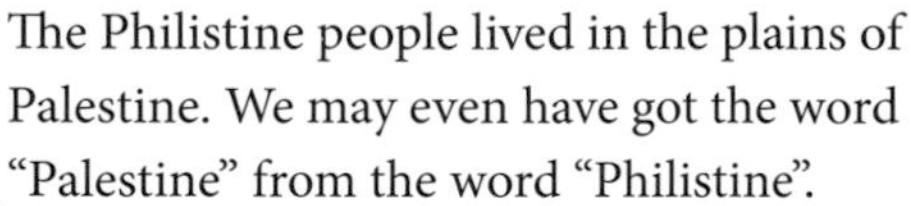

The Philistine people lived in the plains of Palestine. We may even have got the word "Palestine" from the word "Philistine".

These people were more advanced than the Hebrews. They already worked with metal in a way the Hebrews did not. This gave the Philistines an advantage in battle. Perhaps the most famous Philistine was Goliath. But Goliath, for all his might and metal, was killed by a shepherd boy with a sling, showing that when God is on your side, anything can happen. (6:17–18; 13:19–23)

Look out for...

As you read through 1 Samuel, look out for...

Saul. *Sometimes Saul follows God, other times he definitely does not.*

Faithful friendships. *Jonathan's and David's friendship teaches us how to be good friends.*

Study Questions

- What was so bad about having a king in Israel? (8:10–20)
- What did Saul do that made God take away his kingdom? (13:7–14)
- How did Saul's servants describe David? (16:18–19)
- Why were King Saul and his soldiers afraid of Goliath? (17:4–11)
- Why didn't David kill King Saul when he had the chance? (26:5–11)

Philistine warriors had a distinctive headdress. The Philistines had an advantage over the Israelites because they were able to make metal weapons.

2 Samuel

OUTLINE

David becomes king (1–10)

David officially becomes king. Even though Saul tried to kill David, David respects the memory of Saul and his son, Jonathan. David transfers the Ark of the Covenant to the Temple in Jerusalem.

David's sin (11–18)

David sins with Bathsheba, another man's wife. Then he has her husband killed in battle. His life is never the same, as he and his family have to live with the results of what he has done. David's son Absalom plots against him, and David flees from Jerusalem.

David restores his kingdom (19–24)

David has a small band of mighty men who show their loyalty over and over again. Unfortunately, David counts the men of Israel in preparation for war, and lets the numbers go to his head. God disciplines him for his sin of pride.

David's life was so important to Israel that the whole book of 2 Samuel is filled with stories about him.

Most people would expect that David would have been glad when King Saul was finally killed in battle. But David mourned for his king and for his friend Jonathan.

The book of 2 Samuel tells how David became king over Judah and then over all of Israel. Since David followed God's ways in ruling his people, God made David successful. His people loved him and were devoted to him.

David was a good king and military leader. But he made mistakes as a father. Sometimes he did not discipline his children well, which caused him a lot of grief.

David was far from perfect. He committed the serious sins of adultery, deceit, and murder. But when the prophet Nathan told David he was guilty, King David admitted his sin and repented. God forgave David, but 2 Samuel records the lifelong consequences that David and his family suffered.

King David was a skilled musician.

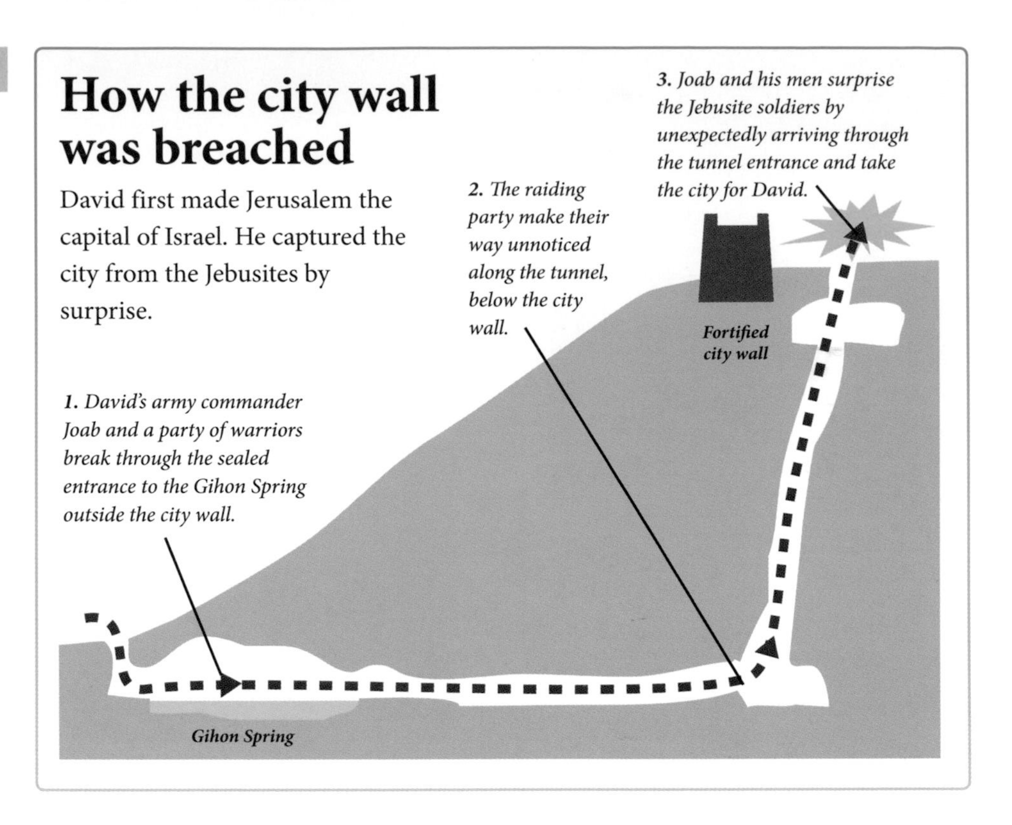

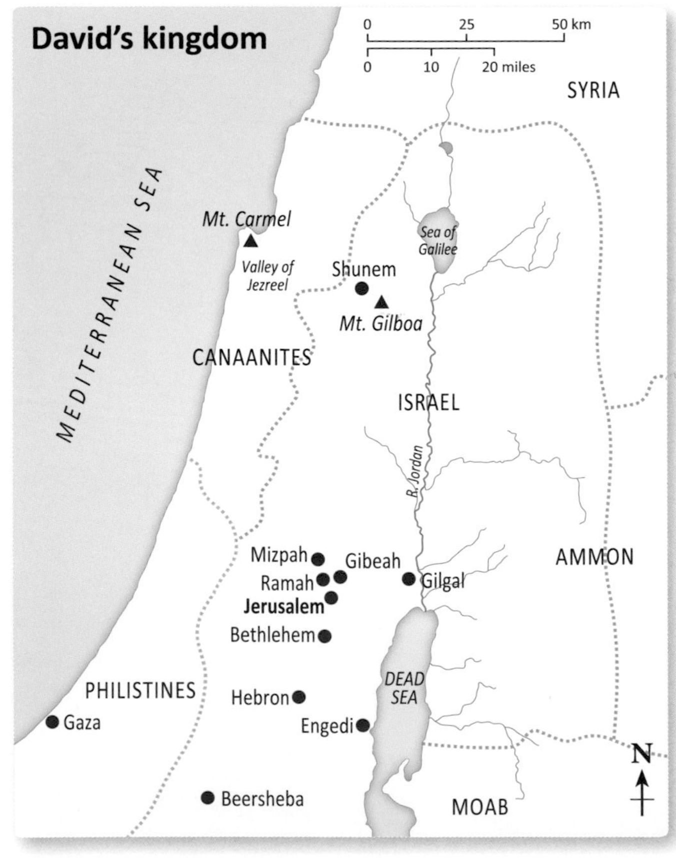

Frequently Asked Questions

Q: How do we know that David was sorry that King Saul was killed?

A: David mourned and fasted because of his grief. He also wrote a lament, or sad song, about King Saul and Jonathan.

Q: What happened to King Saul's family?

A: David was kind to Jonathan's son Mephibosheth. He gave Mephibosheth all Saul's land and let him eat at the king's table.

Q: If David was sorry for his sin, why did God still punish him?

A: God does not take sin lightly. Most of the time sin affects many people, not just the ones who do wrong. By giving in to temptation, David set a bad example for his sons and everyone else.

Ark of the Covenant

A model of the Ark of the Covenant. Two golden cherubim rest on the lid.

The Ark of the Covenant – also called the "Ark of God" and the "Ark of the Lord" – went with the Israelites on all of their journeys. It was like a moving museum. Inside were the tablets on which the Ten Commandments were written. At one time, manna and Aaron's wooden staff were inside too. It was David who finally put the Ark inside the Temple.

The Ark was a sacred object, so God gave strict rules about how it was to be looked after. Normally, no one was to touch it, even by accident. For example, when David was moving the Ark to Jerusalem, a man named Uzzah touched it and fell down dead. Today the location of the Ark is a mystery; it may have been destroyed long ago. (Exodus 25:10–22; Joshua 3–6; 1 Samuel 6:21 – 7:2)

Look out for...

As you read through 2 Samuel, look out for...

Decisions. *David has to make many decisions as king. Most are wise, but some are foolish.*

Consequences. *David makes a few very bad choices. Those choices have consequences, or results, that David has to live through, especially in his family life.*

Crimes. *Several crimes are recorded in 2 Samuel.*

Kindness. *Despite his mistakes, David shows great kindness to several people – far more than people expect.*

Study Questions

- What special promise did God make to David? (7:8–17)
- How did the prophet Nathan draw David's attention to his sin with Bathsheba? (12:1–7)
- How did God punish David for his sin? (12:13–18)
- What sort of men followed King David? (23:8–23)

1 KINGS

The kingdom that David ruled grew even bigger when his son Solomon reigned. 1 Kings tells how Solomon humbly asked God for wisdom to rule. God said he would receive wisdom – and riches and power too. God allowed Solomon to build the beautiful Temple in Jerusalem.

People journeyed great distances to Jerusalem to hear the wise sayings of Solomon. But Solomon forgot God's command not to have many wives (Deuteronomy 17:17). And the wives he married had idols as gods. They turned Solomon's heart away from God.

The rest of this book tells how the nation of Israel was divided into two kingdoms. These were Israel (made up of the ten northern tribes) and Judah (the two southern tribes, Judah and Benjamin).

The people kept turning from God to worship idols. But God did not desert his people. He sent his prophet Elijah to show the people that the Lord is the true God. No matter how wicked the people were, God was always had someone to point the way back to God. The book of 1 Kings is full of examples of people who disobeyed God – and of those who obeyed him.

OUTLINE

The rise of Solomon's kingdom (1–10)

David dies in old age. God offers Solomon anything and is pleased when Solomon asks for wisdom rather than riches or power. Solomon builds the Temple and becomes powerful and rich as well as wise.

The kingdom is divided (11–12)

After Solomon dies, the kingdom divides into northern and southern kingdoms.

Kings and prophets (13–22)

Evil King Ahab lives a life of wickedness. Elijah prophesies to God's people.

The prophet Elijah confronts King Ahab of Israel.

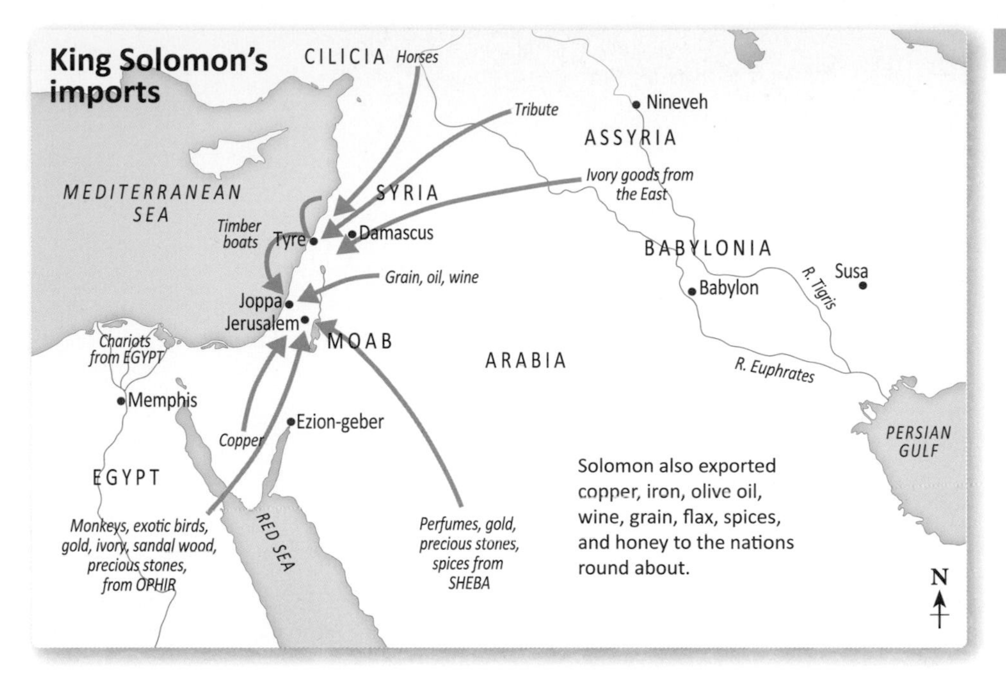

Look out for…

As you read through 1 Kings, look out for…

Choices. *In 1 Kings, it's easy to see that the choices leaders make affect a lot of people.*

Good kings. *The kingdoms of Israel and Judah prosper under godly kings.*

God's care. *God takes care of his people. In 1 Kings, we see how he looks after both Elijah and Elisha.*

Study Questions

- How did God show he was pleased with the Temple that Solomon built? (8:10–13; 9:1–3)
- What caused the kingdom to be divided? (12:1–24)
- Why was King Ahab one of the worst kings of Israel? (16:29–33)
- How did Elijah prove that the Lord is the true God? (18:16–40)

Frequently Asked Questions

Q: Since David had so many sons, how did Solomon become king?

A: Solomon was the one David chose to be king. Bathsheba reminded David that he had promised that her son Solomon would be king. Also God chose Solomon and promised to bless him (1:15–31).

Q: What did God tell Solomon in a dream?

A: God told Solomon to ask for whatever he wanted. God was pleased that Solomon asked for wisdom.

Solomon's Temple

King Solomon's Temple was built with the help of skilled craftsmen from Phoenicia. Like the Tabernacle, it had a larger room at the front, the Holy Place, and a smaller cuboid room behind, the Holiest Place. The Temple was constructed in dressed stone, with cedar and cypress wood panels inside, large areas of which were covered in gold. In the Holy Place stood the altar of incense, the table of the Presence, and the golden lampstand. Inside the dark Holiest Place was the Ark of the Covenant. At the door of the Temple stood two huge pillars, named Jachin and Boaz. In the courtyard in front of the Temple stood a huge bronze "sea", used for ritual cleansing, and a massive altar for burnt offerings.

2 Kings

The book of 2 Kings continues the sad story of the divided kingdom of Israel. It tells of twelve kings of the northern kingdom (called Israel) and sixteen kings of the southern kingdom (Judah). Most of the kings took the evil path, followed idols, and turned away from God. Only a few were good and tried to lead their people back to God.

The northern kingdom lasted only 130 years before Assyria conquered it. But because King Hezekiah and King Josiah obeyed God and the people repented, Judah prospered. God kept Judah safe for another 136 years. However, the evil ways of the people of Judah finally caught up with them. God sent Nebuchadnezzar to take them away into captivity in Babylonia.

During all those years, God sent his prophets to warn the people to return to him. Most people know about Elijah and Elisha. But as many as thirty other prophets also tried to turn people back to God. God always made sure the people would hear his message, so that they could turn back to him.

Relief depicting Sennacherib, King of Assyria 705–681 BC, on his throne. This mighty ruler tried to capture Jerusalem during the reign of King Hezekiah, but failed in the attempt.

Elijah, the bold prophet of Israel who spoke out against Ahab and Jezebel.

OUTLINE

Elijah's final work (1–2)

Elijah is taken into heaven without dying. He passes his power on to Elisha.

Elisha's work (3–13)

Elisha works miracles, including healing Naaman of leprosy. Many kings rule, including Jehu – who kills evil Queen Jezebel and the family of Ahab – and Joash, who repairs the Temple.

Captivity of Israel (14–17)

Israel's kings get worse and worse. They do not obey God who eventually let Israel be captured by the Assyrians.

Captivity of Judah (18–25)

Hezekiah withstands the Assyrians, and Josiah does away with pagan gods. But the Babylonians destroy Jerusalem in 587 BC and take many people into exile.

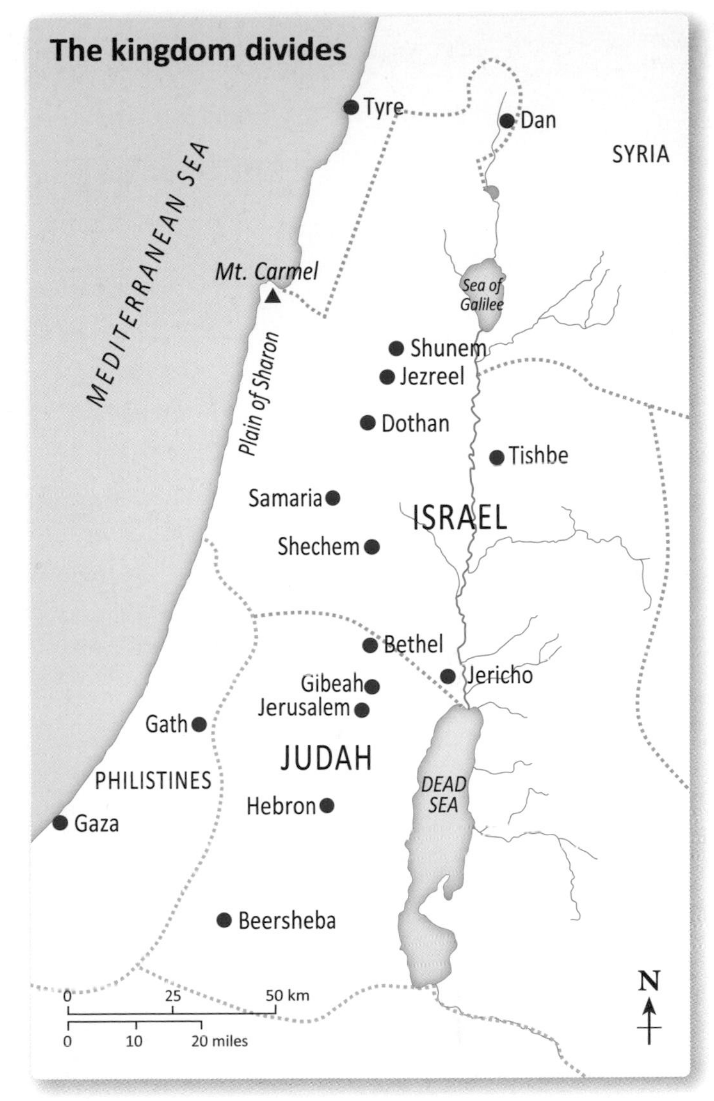

Frequently Asked Questions

Q: Why did the Israelites worship idols?

A: They wanted to be like other nations and do bad things allowed by other nations' religions.

Q: Why was the prophet Elijah so special?

A: Elijah was courageous and stood up against evil King Ahab and Queen Jezebel. He challenged the prophets of Baal and showed the people that the Lord is the true God. God showed his special care for Elijah by not allowing him to die and taking him straight to heaven in a whirlwind instead.

Q: What was so good about Hezekiah and Josiah?

A: These two kings of Judah tried to restore worship of the true God. Hezekiah broke down the places of false worship and destroyed idols. Josiah read God's Word to the people and promised to obey it. The people followed his good example.

Leprosy

Leprosy was a serious skin disease. It was contagious. Anyone who caught it had to leave home, losing his work and family. A man called Naaman was healed of leprosy by washing in the River Jordan (2 Kings 5). Jesus healed people of leprosy more than once.

Old Testament laws taught people how to deal with leprosy. There were certain ways to treat someone with leprosy. Leprosy was such a serious condition that when someone with leprosy saw people approaching, he or she had to yell "Unclean! Unclean!" to warn them not to come near.

Since leprosy was so horrible, it's amazing that Naaman was so reluctant to wash in a river to cure himself. If he had not been so proud, he would have jumped straight in.

Look out for...

As you read through 2 Kings, look out for...

***Kingdoms.** A big change is happening in Israel during this time. Kingdoms are shifting and becoming parts of other kingdoms. Kings change often.*

***Revivals.** Israel and Judah have times of revival, or coming back to God.*

***Pride.** Pride is often a problem in Israel. Naaman struggles with pride. The kings of Israel are often so conceited that they feel no need for God's help.*

Study Questions

- What did Elisha want Elijah to do for him? (2:9–13)
- How did Elisha show that God loves even Israel's enemies? (5:1–16)
- How did King Josiah find the book of the Law? (22:1–20)
- What happened to Jerusalem when the Babylonians captured it? (25:8–10)

1 Chronicles

People like to know where they came from and who their ancestors were. The book of 1 Chronicles gives long lists of people from Adam to Zerubbabel. It shows how God worked in his people's lives for many generations.

There are lists of kings, members of tribes, Temple musicians, priests, people who returned from exile in Babylonia, and David's mighty men.

The book of 1 Chronicles goes with 2 Samuel and fills in many of the details. It was written after the Israelites had been exiled. It doesn't deal with all the kings of Israel and their battles. Instead, it shows how David helped set up worship in Israel, taking the Ark to Jerusalem and preparing to build the Temple. Reading 1 Chronicles is a good way to understand the history of worship in Israel and Judah.

OUTLINE

Genealogies (1–8)

These lists give the history of each of the families (tribes) of Jacob's twelve sons.

Taking back the land (9)

The Israelites had been captives in Babylonia. Now they return to their homeland.

Reign of David (10–21)

David is king of Israel. He returns the Ark of the Covenant to the Temple and wins many battles.

Preparation for the Temple (22–29)

God does not want David to build the Temple, but lets him get all the materials and workers together so Solomon can oversee the building later.

King David led the dance of joy when the Ark of the Covenant was brought to the capital city of Israel, Jerusalem.

Genealogies

The word “genealogy” is similar to the word “generations”. Sometimes, instead of calling a list a “genealogy”, the Bible says, “These are the generations of…” A genealogy is a list of people in a bloodline. It is the history of a family.

The book of 1 Chronicles has the major genealogy of the Old Testament. These lists remind us that the people we read about were real people with families.

Look out for…

As you read through 1 Chronicles, look out for…

Feelings. *1 Chronicles tells about the emotions of people in the story. David is fearful sometimes. At other times he is joyful and full of praise. Like you and me, the people of the Bible have good days and bad days.*

Prayers. *1 Chronicles includes several of David's prayers.*

Lists. *1 Chronicles contains lists of history and descendants (genealogies) as well as lists of warriors and leaders.*

Study Questions

- What lesson did David learn from moving the Ark of God? (13:3–14; 15:1–2)
- What did David say about God's promise to him? (17:16–27)
- How did David help his son Solomon? (22:2–19)

An Israelite warrior.

Frequently Asked Questions

Q: What's so important about this book?
A: This book was useful for the people returning to Jerusalem after being exiled in Babylonia. It helped them know how God had worked in their nation. It encouraged them to trust God and obey him.

Q: Why did David only plan the Temple? Why didn't he build it?
A: David wanted to build the Temple (22:7–8; 28:2–3) but God would not let him. He said David had fought too many battles and killed too many people. So God let Solomon, who lived in peace, build the Temple.

2 Chronicles

OUTLINE

Solomon's reign (1–9)

Solomon asks for wisdom and builds and dedicates the Temple. The queen of Sheba visits.

Kings of Judah (10–36)

The kingdom divides and Judah is ruled by nineteen kings (and a queen), from Rehoboam to Zedekiah. But at God's command, the king of Babylon puts an end to it all.

Though King Solomon was renowned for his wisdom, he later lost his first love for God. High taxes left Israel impoverished and his people angry.

People's lives are filled with many details. 2 Chronicles helps to fill in some facts left out of 1 and 2 Kings. It gives more information about the southern kingdom of Judah. It is the second part of Chronicles, as its name says. (1 and 2 Chronicles used to be a single book.)

2 Chronicles was written to show the importance of worship. It tells how the people of Judah turned back to God and practised their religion sincerely. 2 Chronicles tells the story of Solomon's reign as king. It records how the northern tribes of Israel revolted, led by Jeroboam against Rehoboam, Solomon's son and successor.

It continues to the time when the people of Judah were captured and taken away to Babylonia in 586 BC. By then, the people had stopped obeying God. He allowed the Babylonians to destroy the beautiful Temple that Solomon had built. 2 Chronicles ends by telling how King Cyrus of Persia allowed the people to return to Judah.

Jerusalem: Solomon's Capital City

Although his father, David, first made Jerusalem capital of the kingdom of Israel, Solomon greatly expanded the city, building himself a splendid palace and constructing the Temple, something God did not allow David to do. The original city of David (left) was joined by fortified walls to Solomon's palace complex and the Temple (far right). In the foreground is the Kidron Valley.

KEY EVENTS
The Exile

1. Judah
Through most of Judah's history, God's people turned their backs on God. God warned them many times to turn back to him. (Isaiah 2:5–11)

2. Babylonia
Finally, God sent King Nebuchadnezzar to take the people of Judah captive. He destroyed Jerusalem and took the people to Babylonia. They stayed for seventy years before being allowed to return. (36:15–23)

3. Jerusalem
After many years, Cyrus allowed some exiles to return to Jerusalem to repair the Temple. Zerubbabel led the first group of exiles (Ezra 1:1–8). Years later, Ezra led another group of exiles on the dangerous journey. (Ezra 7:1–10)

Asherah

Asherah was a goddess of the Phoenicians and Syrians. She was also called Ashtoreth, Astarte, Anath, or the Lady of the Sea. The Israelites began to worship Asherah when they turned to idols.

The book of 2 Chronicles mentions "Asherah poles", which were probably statues that were supposed to look like this goddess. Whenever Israel turned away from God, they would put up Asherah poles. When Israel turned back to God, they would pull down the Asherah poles. (15:16–18)

Frequently Asked Questions

Q: Why did God make Solomon so wise?
A: Solomon asked God to make him wise. He did not ask for riches or fame. That pleased God. So God gave him the wisdom he requested, plus riches and respect.

Q: Just how rich was Solomon?
A: During Solomon's reign, his silver and gold were "as common as stones"!

Q: What happened to divide the kingdom?
A: Solomon's son Rehoboam did not listen to the good advice of the older men who had helped Solomon. He listened to young men who said he should be even tougher with the people. That made people very angry. So the ten tribes of the north followed another king instead of Rehoboam.

Look out for...

As you read through 2 Chronicles, look out for...

Wars and invasions. *This is a violent time in Israel's history. There is much in 2 Chronicles about soldiers, invaders, and wars. Usually these conflicts come when the nation is turning from God.*

Acts of unfaithfulness. *Notice how the Israelites change their whole way of living when they turn away from God. Obeying God affects the way we live our lives too.*

Revivals. *When a good and righteous king reigns, he leads the people back to the worship of the one true God. Unfortunately, the people fall back into their old ways as soon as a new king comes along.*

Study Questions

- How did God keep his promise to David? (6:3–11)
- What was Solomon's kingdom like? (9:13–28)
- What did God do when his people turned back to him? (12:1–8; 33:10–13)
- Why did God punish his people? (36:15–16)

Jerusalem in the Time of King Hezekiah

Jerusalem expanded still further during the reign of King Hezekiah. New walls now surrounded the entire city, which occupied both the Eastern and Western Hill. Hezekiah's new city wall was called the "Broad Wall", as it was so wide (6.5 metres/21 feet). Hezekiah also reconstructed the Temple and built a huge platform for it to stand on, and built a new section of the city on the slopes of the Kidron Valley (bottom right).

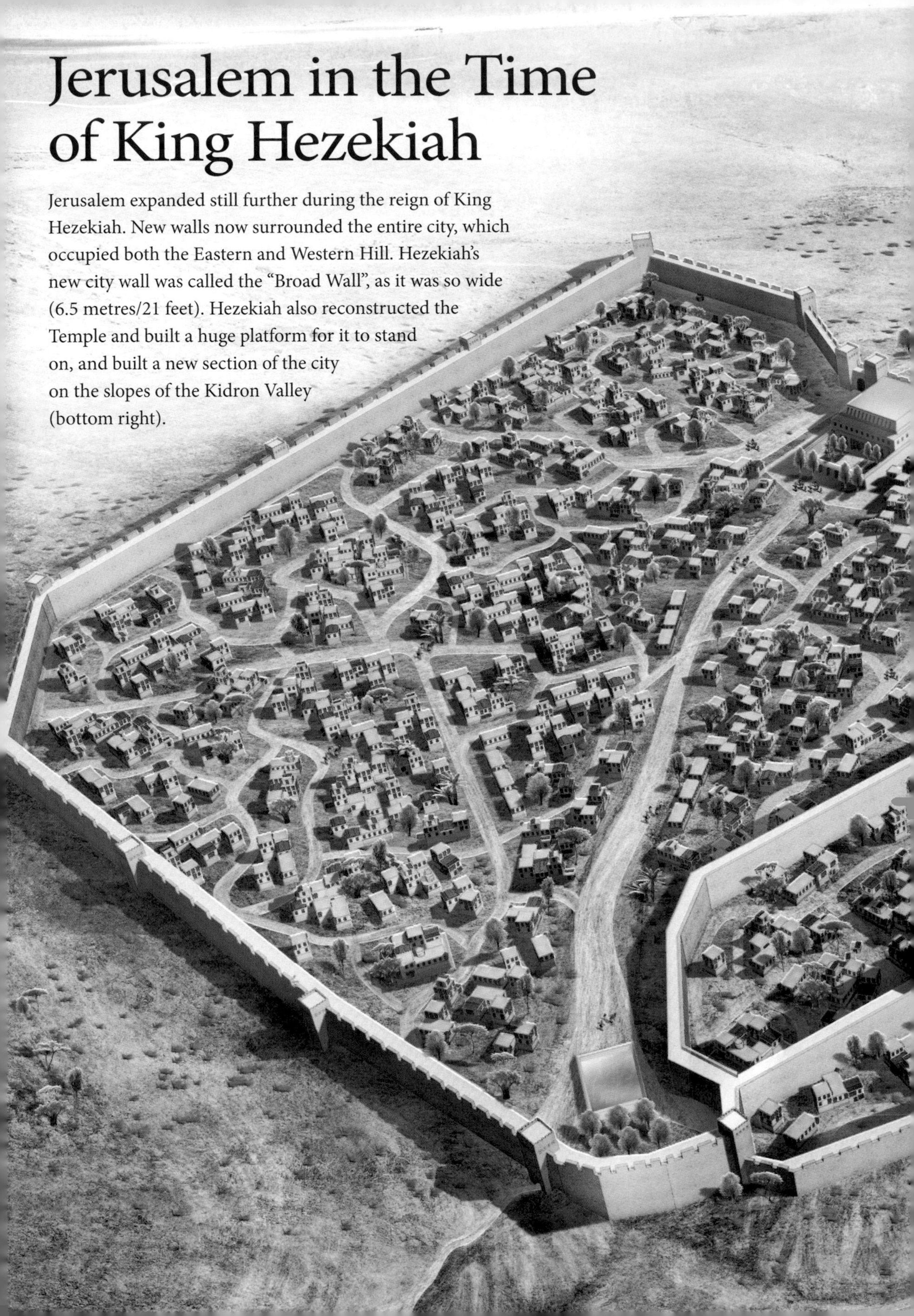

EZRA

Does God use only people who believe in him? The book of Ezra shows how the Lord shapes world events. God had promised his people they would be in captivity in Babylonia for seventy years. When that time was up, God influenced King Cyrus to allow the people to return to Jerusalem.

The book of Ezra describes two groups of Israelites who returned to their country. The first group was led by Zerubbabel. Those who went are listed by family name. More than 42,000 people returned with this first group. With Cyrus's permission, they began to rebuild the Temple soon after they got back to Jerusalem. Others gave them silver, gold, and supplies for the task. But not everyone was happy about this. Some tried to discourage the Jews from working. They said God's people were rebellious and corrupt.

A second group went with Ezra eighty years later, during the reign of King Artaxerxes. The Temple had been rebuilt, but the people were not obeying God. For example, they had married people who had idols for gods. Ezra prayed and helped his people repent of their sin.

OUTLINE

Restoration of worship (1–6)

The first exiles return to Jerusalem and begin to rebuild the Temple. Enemies try to stop them, but the Temple is completed anyway.

Ezra's reforms (7–10)

Ezra arrives and urges the people to obey God wholeheartedly. The people listen to him and change the way they are living.

Ezra reads a letter from King Artaxerxes offering his help in the restoration of the Temple in Jerusalem.

The tomb of Cyrus the Great (559–530 BC), founder of the Persian Empire, at Pasargadae, Iran.

Frequently Asked Questions

Q: Who was Ezra?
A: Ezra was a priest and a scribe. He may be the writer of most of 1 and 2 Chronicles, Ezra, Nehemiah, and Psalm 119. He loved God and wanted his people to obey God. He worked hard to help them understand and obey God's Word.

Q: Why did some of the older people cry when the foundation of the Temple was laid?
A: The older people had seen the glory of Solomon's Temple, and they knew this one would not be so beautiful.

Q: Why didn't Ezra want to ask the king for protection for the trip back to Jerusalem?
A: Ezra had told King Artaxerxes that the Lord takes care of those who trust him. So Ezra prayed for God's protection instead of the king's.

Intermarriage

One of the biggest problems the Jews faced at this time was marrying people who did not love God. God told them not to do this.

The nations around Israel followed false gods. When a Jew married someone who loved idols, they tended to worship those idols instead of the one true God. This was something God would not put up with.

Ezra confronted many priests who had married pagan wives. He listed them all. It took three months to sort it all out. Of all those men, only two refused to obey God. (Chapter 10)

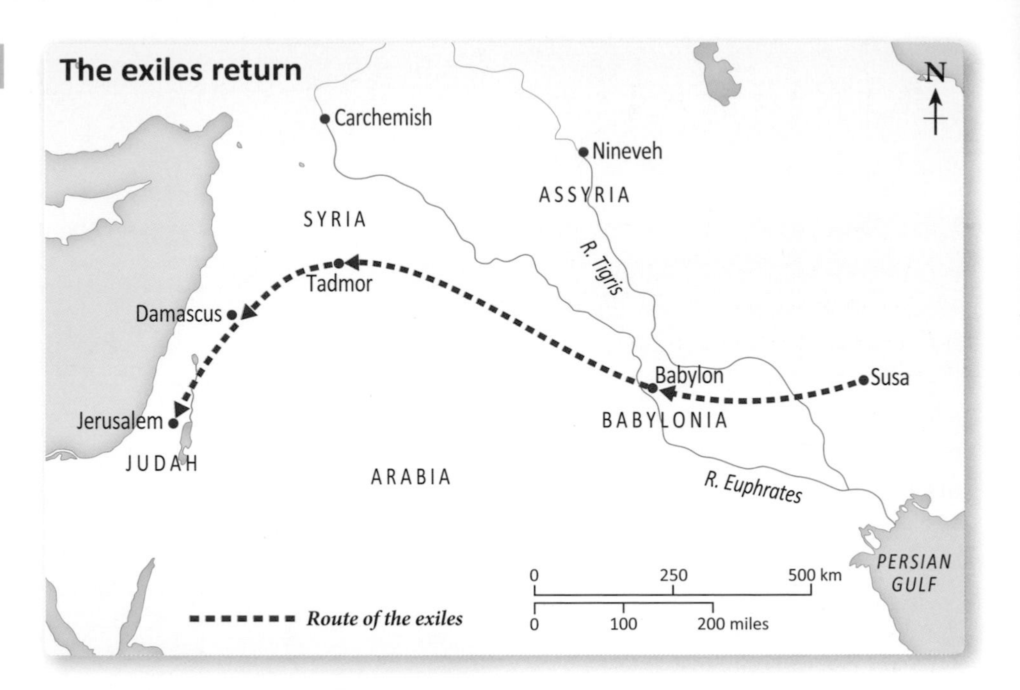

Relief of a Persian chariot.

Study Questions

- How did God use King Cyrus to help the Jewish exiles? (1:2–11)
- What problems did the Jews face while they were rebuilding the Temple? (4:1–5)

Look out for...

As you read through Ezra, look out for...

Exiles. *Exiles are people who are forced to leave their country. In this story, they are Israelites who have been captives in Persia (old Babylonia). They come back to Israel in groups.*

Lists. *Ezra gives several lists: lists of supplies, lists of people returning home, and lists of people caught in sin.*

Proclamations. *Ezra gives us the exact words of several kings. They send out official documents, but since they do not have copiers, one person reads the documents to everyone else. There are messages from three kings: Cyrus, Darius, and Artaxerxes.*

NEHEMIAH

Prayer and action are the key words for the book of Nehemiah. Nehemiah was an Israelite living in exile in Persia (old Babylonia). He was the cup-bearer to King Artaxerxes. This was an important job. Nehemiah heard that the walls of Jerusalem were still broken down after many years. The news made him very sad. He wept and prayed to God. Then he bravely asked Artaxerxes if he could go to Jerusalem and rebuild the walls.

This book shows how Nehemiah prayed, planned, and worked hard. He encouraged the people living in Jerusalem. They needed a strong leader to help them do the work. Enemies did not want the walls to be rebuilt and Nehemiah had to post guards. Many of his men worked with one hand while holding a weapon in the other. Some men even tried to scare Nehemiah. But he continued to trust God and get on with the work.

This book tells of the work Nehemiah and the people did. It also tells about their love for God. Ezra and Nehemiah worked together. Ezra read the book of the Law to the people and helped them learn how God wanted them to live.

The book of Nehemiah tells how the walls of Jerusalem were rebuilt and how the people turned back to God.

Nehemiah oversaw the rebuilding of the walls of Jerusalem.

Nehemiah grew up as a Jewish exile in Babylon, and became cup-bearer to King Artaxerxes of Persia. He led a group of exiles back to Jerusalem to rebuild the ruined city.

Persian palace guards, pictured on glazed bricks from the royal palace of Susa.

OUTLINE

Nehemiah returns to Jerusalem (1–2)

Nehemiah hears that the walls of Jerusalem are broken. He returns to the city and inspects them.

Rebuilding the walls (3–7)

The work begins, with enemies trying to stand in the way. The walls are rebuilt in just fifty-two days.

Revival (8–10)

Ezra reads the book of the Law, and the people repent.

Lists and genealogies (11:1 – 12:26)

The people return to Jerusalem and their homes, organized by family.

Dedication and reform (12:27 – 13:31)

The people dedicate the walls, and Nehemiah begins to change the way they do some things.

Frequently Asked Questions

Q: Why was a cup-bearer important?
A: The cup-bearer was a trusted attendant of the king. He tasted the king's wine first to make sure it was good – and not poisoned! Then he gave it to the king.

Q: Why were the walls of Jerusalem still broken down?
A: People who were not Israelites settled in the land of Judah when the Israelites were taken captive. Those people did not want the Jews (Israelites) to rebuild their city.

Q: What did the Jews do when Nehemiah wanted to rebuild the walls?
A: They were glad to have a leader. They got busy and started work right away.

Festival of Shelters

Reading the Scriptures, Ezra realized that the people were supposed to hold a celebration called the Festival of Shelters. This festival involved making temporary shelters or "booths" to live in for seven days. Ezra and the people were so excited about obeying God that they went straight out and collected branches and leaves to make their shelters. (8:13–18)

The Festival of Shelters (also called "booths" or "tabernacles") was the last sacred festival in the year. It began five days after the Day of Atonement (Leviticus 23:34) and lasted seven days. This festival had two purposes. First, it celebrated the end of the harvest. Second, it reminded the people of the Exodus, when their ancestors had to live in tents.

Look out for...

As you read through Nehemiah, look out for...

Confessions. *When the people read the Law, they are reminded of their sin. Then they confess their sins to God so they can ask him to forgive them.*

Obstacles. *The book of Nehemiah is a story about overcoming obstacles (things that get in your way). Nehemiah has a long journey to make. People try to stop the building of the walls. Some of the people have disagreements. Some of the Jews have a lot of sin in their lives.*

Details. *Nehemiah has a lot of small but important things to take care of, so he has to be very organized. In fact, this book is a great example of organization.*

Study Questions

- How did Nehemiah answer Sanballat and Tobiah when they mocked him? (2:19–20)
- What did Nehemiah and the other Jews do when they were threatened? (Chapter 4)
- How did the people respond to Ezra's reading of God's Word? (8:1–12)

ESTHER

The book of Esther is one of only two books in the Bible named after a woman (the other is Ruth). It tells the story of a young Jewish woman who becomes a queen of Persia. This unusual event was part of God's plan to save the Jewish people in the kingdom of Xerxes (also known as Ahasuerus).

Haman, the prime minister, hated Jews, and especially a man called Mordecai. Haman plotted to have them all killed. He did not know that Queen Esther was Jewish. Mordecai was Esther's cousin. He told Esther about the plot and asked her to help her people.

But although she was queen, Esther could not do whatever she wanted. No one, not even a queen, could speak to the king unless he gave the invitation. Esther told Mordecai to gather all the Jews in the city to fast and pray for her. Then she would approach the king.

Esther needed great courage and wisdom to find a way to speak to the king and turn the evil plot back on Haman. But God helped Esther, and her people were saved! It's an amazing story of God working through his people.

Esther grew up in Susa, the capital of Persia, and was chosen as queen by King Xerxes.

OUTLINE

Queen Vashti is dethroned (1)

Because the queen refuses to appear at the king's party, she loses her position as queen.

Esther becomes queen (2)

Esther's cousin Mordecai enters her in the contest for a queen to replace Vashti. Esther has a year of beauty treatments, then wins the king's heart and becomes his wife. She does not tell him she is a Jew, because the Jews are captives.

Haman's plans are overturned (3–7)

Haman starts to resent Mordecai, because Mordecai does not show him enough respect. Haman plans to do away with Mordecai and get rid of all the Jews. But Esther is one step ahead of him and asks the king to protect her people. The king falls out with Haman, who is executed.

The Jews celebrate their deliverance (8–9)

Esther tells the people to celebrate the feast of Purim to remember God's deliverance.

Mordecai is promoted (10)

The king realizes what a useful man Mordecai is and gives him an important position in the kingdom.

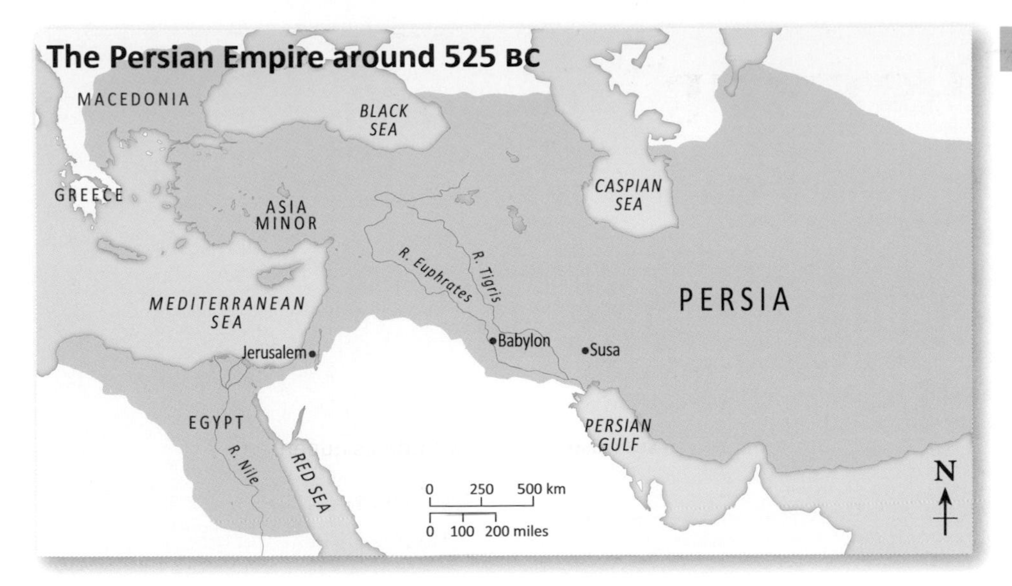

Frequently Asked Questions

Q: How did Esther become queen?

A: The king wanted a new queen. He had all the beautiful young women come to his palace. Esther won his love and he chose her as his queen.

Q: Why did no one know Esther was Jewish?

A: Mordecai told Esther not to talk about her race or her background.

Q: Why did Haman hate Mordecai?

A: Haman was descended from the royal line of the Amalekites, old enemies of the Jews. Mordecai refused to bow down to Haman.

Q: Why was it such a big deal for Esther to talk to the king?

A: The law said that no one could approach the king unless the king invited that person to come. Anyone who disobeyed this law and came uninvited was put to death. Only if the king held out his golden rod would the person be spared.

Look out for...

As you read through Esther, look out for...

Opportunities. *Esther, Mordecai, and Haman all have opportunities to do something – some good and some bad. Watch for what they do with their opportunities.*

Deceit and pride. *A lot of Haman's actions come from his pride and deceit.*

Social customs. *Many social customs of the Persians are found in this book. For example, the beauty contest for queen, the way people get to talk to the king, dinner arrangements, and the festivals all tell something about the people of that time and place.*

Study Questions

- What did Haman do when he found out Mordecai was a Jew? (3:5–14)
- What happened to Haman when the king understood his plot? (7:9–10)

Job

Job had a great fortune, measured by his vast possessions, which included 7,000 sheep and 3,000 camels.

The story of Job brings up questions about why humans suffer.

Good people never have problems, right? Wrong! The book of Job is about a very good man named Job. God described him as "blameless", a man who loved God and "stayed away from evil". But Job had more trouble in one day than most people have in a lifetime. In fact, Job had so much trouble that no one could comfort him.

God pointed out Job as a good example of a follower of God. But Satan ("the Accuser") said Job just loved God for what he could get for himself. Not so, said God, and gave Satan permission to test Job.

In one day, Job's ten children were killed, his servants were killed, and all his wealth was destroyed or stolen. Satan expected Job to curse God. Instead, Job still loved God!

Next Satan wanted to test Job by hurting his body. God gave Satan permission to hurt Job, but not to kill him. Satan made painful sores appear all over Job's body.

Job felt very miserable. He could not understand why God was allowing all this to happen to him. But he never cursed God.

Some of Job's friends visited him. At first they just sat with him and kept him company. Later they argued with him that all his trouble was caused by his sin. But Job had not sinned – and he knew it.

God did not answer Job's questions. But he helped Job see that God is in control – even when bad things happen to good people.

OUTLINE

Satan tests Job (1–2)

Satan comes to God and asks permission to test Job.

Job and his friends discuss his suffering (3–31)

Job and three friends talk about his suffering and why it is happening. Most of their answers upset Job instead of comforting him. They think Job has done something wrong to deserve what is happening.

Elihu speaks (32–37)

Elihu does not blame Job, but reminds him that God does things which people cannot always understand.

God speaks (38–41)

God speaks to Job and sets the record straight. He shows Job how wrong his three friends are.

Job's reply and conclusion (42)

Job admits that God's ways are hard to understand. But he still believes God is good. God corrects Job's friends and then gives Job more than he had before.

Frequently Asked Questions

"God cannot be seen – but his power is great, and he is always fair." (37:23, CEV)

Q: Why did Satan have power to hurt Job?
A: God let Satan do it. God gave Satan special permission to test Job's faith.

Q: Does Satan cause all suffering?
A: No. People can make good or bad choices. Bad choices can cause trouble for them and others. Also, sometimes God allows and uses hard things to help our faith grow stronger.

Q: Why did Job's friends think he had sinned?
A: They thought that bad things only happen to bad people. Even Job was confused. He knew he had not sinned, so he did not know why he was "being punished".

Suffering

To suffer means to have bad things happen to you. People have faced suffering since Adam and Eve were thrown out of Eden.

Often people think suffering is a punishment from God for doing wrong. All of Job's friends thought this. Even Jesus' disciples thought this. But no one can know why God allows this or that bad thing to happen. And we should never assume we do know.

Jesus and his disciples met a man who had been blind from birth (John 9:1–3). The disciples immediately asked, "Why did this happen? Did this man sin or did his parents?" Jesus told his disciples that the man's blindness was not a punishment from God at all. It was an opportunity for people to see him healed by God and be amazed at God's power and love.

Bad things happen to people. Even though we may want to blame someone, or ask God why, we may not get an answer. Whenever we suffer we should do what Job did. We should praise God because we know he is with us and has a plan for our lives.

Study Questions

- What bad advice did Job's wife give him? (2:9)
- What effect did God's words have on Job? (42:1–6)
- How did God feel about Job's friends? (42:7–9)
- What did God do for Job after Job prayed for his friends? (42:10–17)

Look out for…

As you read through Job, look out for…

Losses. *Job loses almost everything. Can you think of anything he doesn't lose?*

Arguments. *As Job and his friends talk, they are almost arguing, not because they are angry but because they are trying to work all this out.*

Job defending himself. *Job is brave enough to stand up to his friends. He has done nothing wrong to deserve such suffering, and he's brave enough to say it.*

PSALMS

Sometimes people don't say what they're really thinking. But the psalms are not like that – they say it just like it is. They have joyful praise to the Lord. They have mournful sorrow for sin. They have prayer for direction and comfort. They have requests to punish people who reject God.

Some psalms cry out for help in hard places. Others ask God for daily needs to be met. And there are prayers for forgiveness.

The psalms were written by different people. Some are for public worship. Some are private thoughts written when people were discouraged.

There are 150 psalms. They were written by David, Asaph, the sons of Korah, Solomon, Heman, Ethan, Moses, and others. Some have no known author. They teach many things – about God the Creator, his power, and his faithfulness. Many speak of Jesus in the future.

Psalms are actually songs to be sung. The book of Psalms was the hymn book of the Jews. Over the years, many psalms have been put to music for Christians to sing.

Look out for...

As you read through Psalms, look out for...

Instruments. *The psalms mention many musical instruments, such as lyres and tambourines. Some of the instruments you read about in the book of Psalms are still in use today.*

Composers. *Many psalms name their writer. You will see different names, but many are by King David.*

Praise. *A great theme of the psalms is praise. Songs or psalms help us praise God joyfully for our lives and all good things.*

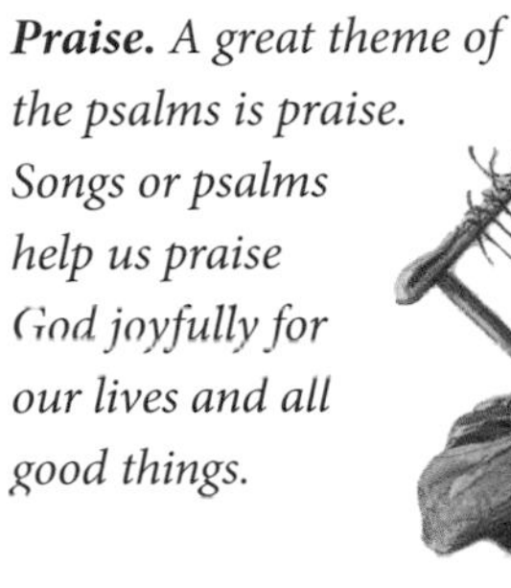

An Israelite musician plays on his lyre.

A shepherd in Israel looks after his flock.

Frequently Asked Questions

Q: If the psalms are songs, why don't they rhyme?
A: Hebrew poetry is different from English poetry. It doesn't rhyme. Instead, the second line often repeats the first line using different words. In fact, almost all Hebrew poetry uses two lines to make its point. The first line says something, and then the second line says it again in a different way. Sometimes each line begins with the next letter of the alphabet.

Q: Why did David pray to God to punish his enemies?
A: David and the other writers of the psalms were people just like you and me; they told God exactly how they felt. They also knew that God is in control, so they asked him to change things. That's how we should pray too.

Psalm 23

The Lord is my shepherd,
I lack nothing.
He makes me lie down in green
pastures,
he leads me beside quiet waters,
he refreshes my soul.
He guides me along the right paths
for his name's sake.
Even though I walk
through the darkest valley,
I will fear no evil,
for you are with me;
your rod and your staff,
they comfort me.
You prepare a table before me
in the presence of my enemies.
You anoint my head with oil;
my cup overflows.
Surely your goodness and love will
follow me all the days of my life,
and I will dwell in the house of the
Lord forever.

NIV

Replica musical instruments of Bible times.

Musical instruments

Many musical instruments are listed in the psalms. You'll recognize some, such as bells and cymbals and flutes. Although some of the names are the same, the instruments have changed.

The Jews used a tambourine in their worship services. But these tambourines did not have the metal pieces along the side that make the jingle noises. They were like small, handheld drums. The harps were smaller than harps today, and had only ten strings. The trumpets were long ram's horns or metal horns, but did not have valves to push with your fingers to make different sounds.

There were also instruments with completely different names, although we have something like them. Sistrums were shakers that were held in your hand. A lyre was a small harp. It was played with a plectrum, or kind of pick.

The people of Israel used many other musical instruments too. Music has always been an important part of worship.

Study Questions

- How does David describe someone who pleases God? (Psalm 15)
- What does David say about a person who asks for God's forgiveness? (Psalm 32)
- What are some of the ways in which people can praise God? (Psalm 150)

Proverbs

No one wants to be called foolish. The book of Proverbs can help make people wise. It is a source of wisdom. Most of it was written by Solomon, the wisest king of Israel. Solomon wrote these wise sayings and rules for living, especially for God's people. But God has given them to everyone who wants to know how to live wisely.

The truly wise person wants to know and love God. A wise person learns how to live peacefully with family, friends, and other people.

The book of Proverbs is written in Hebrew poetry. It is not the kind of poetry that rhymes. Instead, the lines are in couplets, or double lines. The lines are joined with words such as "but" or "and". For example, Proverbs 10:8 says, "The wise are glad to be instructed, but babbling fools fall flat on their faces."

"Good people have kind thoughts." (12:5, CEV)

Proverbs covers every subject you can imagine to do with living. It tells us how to use money, and how not to use it. It tells us the difference between foolishness and wisdom. It tells us how to succeed. It tells us what's right and what's wrong. It even tells us what God loves and hates.

The proverbs are important for everyone who wants to make good decisions.

OUTLINE

This book is filled with short verses about a lot of different things. Here are the main topics:

Advice for getting wisdom (1–9)
Also warnings against foolishness.

Instructions on good living (10–16)
Including advice for families.

Advice for increasing wisdom, understanding, and learning (17–24)
Including thirty wise sayings (22:17 – 24:30).

Instructions and warnings about rejecting the truth (25–29)
Plenty of good sense!

Examples of wonderful, wise, and foolish things (30–31)
Includes a famous passage on the good wife (31:10–31).

Discipline

Proverbs has a lot to say about discipline. It says that parents should discipline their children, that people should discipline themselves, and that God disciplines us. So what is discipline?

Discipline is not punishment. God disciplines us by doing something in our life that makes us stop and think, so that we can make better choices. We discipline ourselves when we control ourselves, instead of doing whatever we want, whenever we want, no matter whether it's right or wrong.

Proverbs says over and over again that discipline is a good thing. We should be open to it and appreciate it.

Look out for...

As you read through Proverbs, look out for...

Lazy people. *Proverbs has a lot to say about people who are not willing to work.*

Wisdom. *Proverbs is a book about getting wisdom and then living by it. Since God made Solomon very wise, it makes sense that Solomon wrote a book about wisdom.*

Family guidelines. *Many verses are about how parents should treat their children, and how children should treat their parents.*

Frequently Asked Questions

Q: Who else wrote some of the proverbs besides Solomon?

A: Other people mentioned as authors of proverbs are Agur and Lemuel.

Q: What made Solomon so wise?

A: When Solomon began to reign as king, God asked him what he wanted. Solomon asked for wisdom. God answered his prayer.

Q: Wasn't Solomon foolish in having a lot of wives?

A: Yes, but he wrote these wise sayings early in his reign, when he was still seeking wisdom from God.

"All wisdom comes from the Lord, and so do common sense and understanding." (2:6, CEV)

Study Questions

- What is the purpose of the proverbs? (1:1–6)
- Why is it important to guard your heart? (4:23)
- How did Jesus use the proverbs? (25:6–7; Luke 14:7–11)

ECCLESIASTES

"I had more sheep and goats than anyone who had ever lived in Jerusalem." *(2:7, CEV)*

Sometimes people say that experience is the best teacher. But learning from another person's mistakes is even wiser. Solomon wrote Ecclesiastes at the end of his life. If we follow his advice, the things he wrote can help us be wise.

Solomon, the most glorious king of Israel, had everything his heart could desire. But he realized that nothing can give happiness if a person doesn't know God.

Solomon, or "the preacher", said that apart from God, everything is in vain. If a person is very popular but not a good friend, they will be lonely. If someone has a great job but works only for himself or herself, the job has no purpose. Even expensive cars, big houses, nice clothes, pretty jewels, money to travel, and great knowledge won't make a person happy, apart from God.

God made people spiritual beings. We need to know God in order for life to have real meaning.

OUTLINE

Riches, success, and prosperity don't make us happy (1:1 – 5:12)

Solomon had all this and more, but without obeying God he was still miserable.

Possessions usually make life harder – not easier (5:13 – 6:12)

We think that the more we have the happier we will be. But things do not bring happiness.

People don't know what's best for them (7–11)

Because we don't really know what's best for us, we make bad choices. We need God to help us make better choices.

One way to live (12)

Fearing and obeying God is the only meaningful way to live.

Look out for...

As you read through Ecclesiastes, look out for...

"Under the sun." *Solomon uses this phrase a lot.*

Achievements and riches. *Solomon is not shy about telling us what he has done and what he has gained.*

Happiness. *Ecclesiastes talks about happiness more than any other book in the Bible. Notice what kinds of things make people happy or unhappy.*

Frequently Asked Questions

Q: What kind of things did Solomon have?
A: Solomon was wealthy. He had delicious food, expensive clothes, a large palace, slaves, attendants, horses and chariots, and beautiful gardens. He was very popular. People visited him from other countries to hear his wisdom. He lived in peace and ease. He had many beautiful wives and children.

Q: Why wasn't Solomon happy?
A: Solomon forgot to stay close to God. Without living for the true God, he couldn't find peace – no matter how much stuff he had.

Study Questions

- What good advice did Solomon give to young people? (12:1)
- Why should people study Solomon's wise sayings? (12:9–11)
- What are Solomon's final, most important words of advice? (12:13–14)

Meaninglessness

Ecclesiastes talks a lot about what is meaningless. (Some Bibles use the word "vanity" or "futile" instead of "meaningless".) All these words mean "empty"; something that does not have a reason or purpose. Some Bibles use the phrase "chasing after the wind". It is silly to chase the wind because you can never catch it.

Solomon wrote this when he was old. He was probably looking back at things he once thought were important, but now realized that only his relationships with people and with God were important.

Solomon wrote a lot about this because he wanted his life to matter. That's how we all are. We want our lives to matter. We want to do something important that makes a difference. We don't want to waste our lives. Over and over again, Solomon reminds us that if we want our lives to matter we need to build a strong friendship with God and live our lives for him. Solomon also says we need to enjoy this life that God has given us. Then, when we are old, we will not feel as if we have wasted our lives.

King Solomon.

Song of Songs

The Song of Songs is a love song written by King Solomon. (In some Bibles it's called the "Song of Solomon".) It tells about his love for his wife and of his wife's love for him. It celebrates their love for each other and the way it brought them together. It shows that love kept them together too.

God invented the special love that makes a marriage work. In God's plan, marriage is very important. It gives people companionship, pleasure, and a safe place to raise a family. This song tells about two people falling in love, marrying, and growing in their love for each other. The words are powerful, because true love is a great thing.

OUTLINE

All the ways they love each other (1:2 – 3:5)

People who love each other give each other compliments. That's what these two people are doing.

The marriage (3:6 – 5:1)

Solomon marries his bride.

The wife misses her husband (5:2 – 6:3)

The woman goes searching for her husband because she loves him so much.

The beauty of the Shulammite bride (6:4 – 7:9)

This young king talks again about how beautiful his wife is.

The wonder of love (7:10 – 8:14)

A stone vineyard watchtower in Israel.

Look out for…

As you read through the Song of Songs, look out for…

Compliments. *When people are in love, they can't say enough good things about each other. That's how this couple is.*

Comparisons. *Often in the Song of Songs the writer compares one thing to another. He says, "She is as fair as the moon." She says, "His eyes are like doves." They find wonderful things around them and compare these wonderful things to the person they love.*

A bride in traditional headdress.

Gazelle

A gazelle, or roe, is the same kind of animal as an antelope or a deer. It runs fast and can live well in the desert. It is sure-footed and can make its way quickly over rough ground.

The gazelle is a beautiful animal too. It moves with grace and elegance. That's why it's used to describe beauty in the Song of Songs.

Frequently Asked Question

Q: Why is this book in the Bible?

A: It shows how important it is for husbands and wives to love each other. It also shows that marriage is God's idea – and a pretty good one too!

Study Questions

- What's so special about love? (8:6–7)
- What advice about love did Solomon's wife have for her friends? (2:7; 3:5; 8:4)

ISAIAH

Some people want to know the future. But many go to the wrong place to find out what's going to happen. They go to fortune tellers. God said not to do that. Instead, God sent prophets to tell the people of Israel the future.

One of the greatest prophets was Isaiah. His prophecies usually had a double message. Something would happen soon after the prophet spoke. Then a second, fuller event would take place hundreds of years later. Some of those events are still in the future.

Isaiah's prophecies were written down in the book of Isaiah. Many of the things Isaiah spoke about concerned the coming of the Messiah, Jesus.

The book of Isaiah is divided into two parts. The first part was to warn Judah, Israel, and nearby nations. God was going to punish them for their sin. Unfortunately, people did not pay attention to Isaiah's warnings. The second part of Isaiah is full of words of comfort: the promise of forgiveness is found in the Messiah. People can find hope in this promise today.

The prophet Isaiah preached mainly to Judah.

OUTLINE

God judges Israel and Judah (1–12)

Israel and Judah have become sinful nations.

God judges foreign nations (13–23)

Prophecies against Babylon, Assyria, Philistia, Moab, Damascus, Egypt, and Tyre.

Prophecies of end times (24–35)

Isaiah describes a period of dreadful punishment as well as the future reign of Christ.

History (36–39)

Sennacherib invades. Hezekiah is sick. Isaiah predicts that the Babylonians will invade.

A book of consolation (40–66)

Prophecies of redemption and restoration bring comfort to the Jewish people who are in exile in Babylonia.

Frequently Asked Questions

Q: Who was Isaiah?
A: Isaiah was an Israelite prophet, the son of Amoz. Isaiah married a prophetess. They had two sons. Isaiah was probably brought up in an upper-class home. He preached mainly to Judah. He was a writer and messenger to four kings (not counting the Assyrian king Sennacherib).

Q: How did Isaiah know he was supposed to be a prophet?
A: Isaiah saw God on his throne in the Temple. When Isaiah saw his sinfulness next to God's holiness, he was afraid. But God forgave him. Then God asked who would go to the people for him. Isaiah said he would go.

Q: Why did God want Isaiah to be a prophet?
A: The people were disobeying God. They were turning to idols and even sacrificing their children to false gods. God was going to punish his people for their wickedness. But he wanted Isaiah to speak to them so they would turn back to God and not suffer.

Study Questions

- What was it like for Isaiah to see God? (6:1–8)
- What are some of the best-known prophecies about the Messiah? (7:14; 9:6–7; 53:1–12)

Relief of Sargon II of Assyria (722–705 BC), who made war on Israel (see Isaiah 20:1).

Look out for...

As you read through Isaiah, look out for...

Descriptions of God. *Isaiah uses many titles and descriptions for God. Each is filled with awe and respect.*

Salvation. *Isaiah explains salvation in many ways, including word pictures. He uses a range of images, such as water and white wool.*

The Messiah. *Isaiah says a lot about the Messiah. One of the most famous passages is chapter 53.*

Babylon

Babylon was the capital of a country with almost the same name, Babylonia. The city was sited on the Euphrates River. One of Babylon's most famous rulers was Nebuchadnezzar (Nebuchadrezzar II). During his reign more than fifty temples to false gods stood in the city.

Nebuchadnezzar probably built the famous Hanging Gardens that were one of the Seven Wonders of the World (bottom right). Other famous features of Babylon include the Ishtar Gate, with its surface of blue glazed tiles, leading to the Processional Way; the great Ziggurat which dominated the city; and the Temple of Marduk. The palace of Nebuchadnezzar is the large wedge-shaped building between the Ziggurat and the Ishtar Gate.

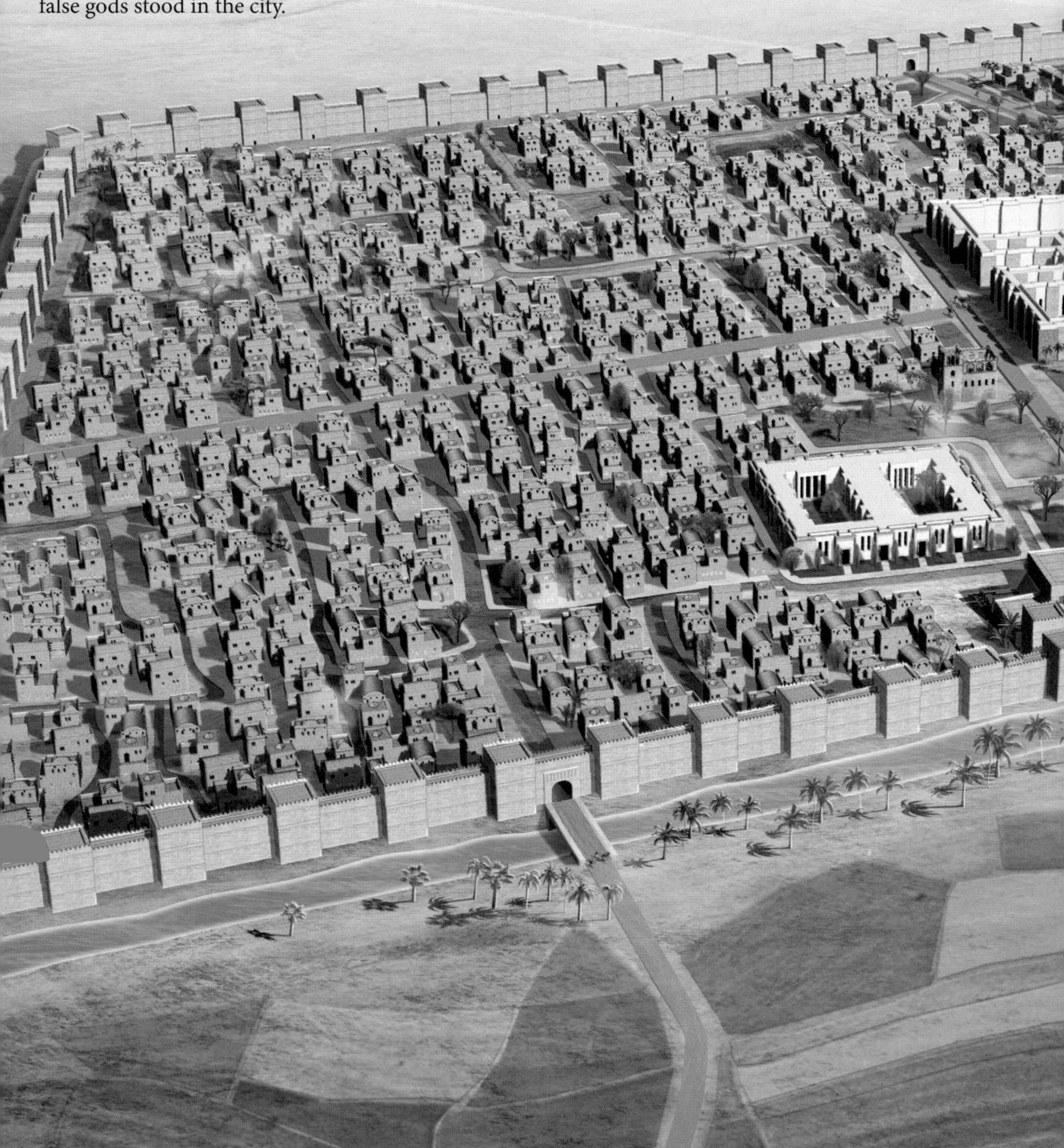

Some of the Israelites taken into exile went to Babylon. Daniel was one of the most famous Israelites in the capital city. He was there while Nebuchadnezzar, Darius, and Cyrus were rulers.

Eventually, the Jews were allowed to return to their homeland. After some time, Babylon began to decline. Today it is an abandoned city, buried under sand in the desert of Iraq. Some parts of it have been dug up, but its glory has vanished.

JEREMIAH

Most people don't want to hear bad news. But the prophet Jeremiah had a lot of bad news to tell his people. They were turning away from the true God and following false gods. God told Jeremiah to warn them that punishment was coming soon.

Jeremiah spoke to ordinary people, false prophets, priests, and kings. Baruch, his secretary, wrote down the words that Jeremiah received from God. But the people wouldn't listen to Jeremiah. One king even burned the scroll on which Jeremiah had written God's message. Jeremiah and Baruch just made another one!

On one occasion, God used a branch of almond blossom to remind Jeremiah that what he tells the prophet will actually happen. (1:11–12)

The coming punishment was fierce. It was so bad that God told Jeremiah not to marry. God did not want Jeremiah to have a wife and children who would suffer the terrible times that were approaching.

Jeremiah prophesied for forty years. Very few people listened to him in all that time. He was rejected by almost everyone.

But Jeremiah's prophecies came true, just as God had said they would. Jerusalem was destroyed by the Babylonian king Nebuchadnezzar and his army – just as God had warned.

Thankfully, God also promised that one day Judah would be restored through the Messiah.

OUTLINE

The book of Jeremiah is not in chronological order. It describes true events, but not in the order that they happened.

Prophecies against Judah and Israel (1–20)

Jeremiah describes how God called him, and then gives several visions (or "oracles") threatening sinful nations with captivity.

History (21–45)

The decline and fall of Jerusalem.

Prophecies against other nations (46–51)

Prophecies against Egypt, Philistia, Moab, Ammon, Edom, Damascus, Elam, and Babylon.

Exiled to Babylonia (52)

Jerusalem falls and the people are taken away from their homes. This is to punish them for their worship of idols.

Study Questions

- What did God say are the important things in life? (9:23–24)
- What happened to Jeremiah and his friend Ebed-melech when Nebuchadnezzar captured Jerusalem? (Chapter 39)

Potters

In chapter 18, Jeremiah compares God to a potter and people to clay. Potters in Jerusalem found their own clay and removed any stones from it. Then they shaped the clay on a wooden wheel. After the pottery was the right shape, they baked it until it was hard.

If the potter went wrong during the shaping, he would simply smash the pot and shape it again. If the pot broke after it had been baked, the potter would throw the pieces into a potter's field (Matthew 27:7, 10).

Look out for...

As you read through Jeremiah, look out for...

***Sins.** Jeremiah is so sad about his nation's sin that he talks about it many times.*

***Jerusalem.** The book has two descriptions of the fall of Jerusalem.*

***Forgiveness.** Jeremiah speaks about sin a lot, but he also says that God forgives us when we repent.*

Frequently Asked Questions

Q: What made Jeremiah so brave?
A: God told Jeremiah he had chosen him for the special task of prophet. He told Jeremiah not to be afraid. God promised to be with him and protect him.

Q: Didn't anyone listen to Jeremiah in forty years?
A: A few did, for example, Baruch, Jeremiah's scribe, or secretary, and some palace officials who warned the king not to burn the scroll. Ebed-melech, another official, spoke up for Jeremiah when others wanted to kill him. But mostly the people didn't listen.

LAMENTATIONS

Assyrian relief picturing captives being taken into exile.

Jeremiah was right, but he wasn't glad about it. He told the king of Judah and the people that God would punish them for their sins. God did as he said. God sent the Babylonians to destroy the city of Jerusalem. They captured the people and took them away to Babylonia.

But Jeremiah wasn't happy to be right. He was very sad. So he wrote the book of Lamentations.

Lamentations consists of five sad poems. It tells about all the bad things that happened to Jerusalem and the people. It describes God's anger at the sin of Judah. Jeremiah speaks of his sorrow and tears for his people. He had warned them and wanted them to turn to God. But they did not repent, and paid the price.

But in the midst of all the sadness, Jeremiah wrote that people can have hope in God. Jeremiah also assures us that God does not give up on his people. God draws people back to himself.

OUTLINE

The loneliness of Zion (1)

Jerusalem used to be a beautiful and powerful city, but now is weak and gets taken over by another nation.

God's anger against the people of Jerusalem (2)

God is finally going to punish the Israelites for their wickedness.

Jeremiah's grief (3)

Jeremiah tells God how sad he is. Then Jeremiah remembers that God is faithful.

Confession and prayers for mercy (4–5)

Jeremiah prays that his people will be restored.

Jerusalem

Jerusalem was a walled city. In the time of Jeremiah, the walls of a city were up to 9 metres (30 feet) thick, so it was no small thing that the walls of Jerusalem were torn down. The present walls extend for 4 kilometres (2.5 miles) and have an average height of 12 metres (40 feet).

Gates were built into the walls. Jerusalem has eight gates now, but they are not all in use. In Jeremiah's day, the gates were closed at night or in times of danger.

Jerusalem was also the capital of Judah and the home of the Temple built by King Solomon. Jerusalem was where the death, resurrection, and ascension of Jesus took place. It was the most important city to the Jews. So when Jeremiah wept over Jerusalem, he was weeping for the whole nation.

A Jewish young man prays at the Western Wall, Jerusalem, the only part of the Temple which still stands today.

Look out for...

As you read through Lamentations, look out for...

Sadness. *Jeremiah is very sad about the sins of his people.*

Prayers. *Often Jeremiah suddenly starts to pray in the middle of his story of the downfall of Jerusalem.*

Consequences. *In Lamentations, the people of Israel are suffering the results of their sin.*

Frequently Asked Questions

Q: Why didn't Jeremiah tell the Israelites, "I told you so!"?

A: Jeremiah loved his people and the city of Jerusalem. He loved God too. He wanted the people to love God and enjoy his blessings. He was truly sorry that they disobeyed God and suffered for it.

Q: Why did Jeremiah cry?

A: Jeremiah cried because terrible things happened to his people. Their homes were ruined. Families were broken up. People were killed. Others were taken away to a foreign country. The city and the Temple were destroyed. Jeremiah had many reasons to cry.

Study Questions

- What was it like for the people when Jerusalem was destroyed? (2:11–12)
- What words of hope did Jeremiah have? (3:22–23, 31–33)

EZEKIEL

While Jeremiah spoke to the people in Jerusalem, Ezekiel spoke to the Jews exiled in Babylonia. Ezekiel was younger than Jeremiah. The book of Ezekiel tells about Ezekiel's work as a prophet and his message to the exiles.

Ezekiel had been taken captive with King Jehoiachin. God used Ezekiel as an example to show the exiles what would happen to them. For example, God told him to lie on his side for 390 days – one day for each year that the Israelites sinned (4:5). Ezekiel delivered God's messages to his people.

Ezekiel said that God was right to punish the Israelites because they were so wicked. He also gave hope to the people. God gave Ezekiel a vision of a valley full of dry bones that became living people. This was a promise that the nation of Israel would be fully restored. God promised to take away their "heart of stone" and give them a "new heart" (36:26).

One time God told Ezekiel to build a dirt mound, to represent an enemy attack on Jerusalem, as a warning to the people of Israel.

OUTLINE

Warnings to Israel (1–24)

Ezekiel is called by God to be a prophet. He starts to warn the Jews that God will punish their sin. He prophesies that Babylon will attack Jerusalem. It happens just as he said it would.

Warnings to nations surrounding Israel (25–32)

Ezekiel gives messages to the nations around Israel because they have treated God's people badly.

Visions of the future (33–48)

Ezekiel sees bones coming back to life and begins to prophesy that God's people will be restored.

Look out for...

As you read through Ezekiel, look out for...

Prophecy. *Ezekiel prophesies about many things that have already come true, and many that are still going to happen.*

Repentance. *Ezekiel calls on his own people as well as foreigners to repent.*

Visions. *Ezekiel has several visions that help him understand what God wants to do.*

Egypt

Egyptian warriors, from an ancient Egyptian wall painting.

The book of Ezekiel mentions Egypt many times. Egypt was and is a country south-west of Israel. Moses led the people of Israel out of slavery in Egypt.

The Nile is a famous river in Egypt. It is so important to that dry, desert country that in the past the people regarded the river as a god. There are also a lot of famous sights in Egypt, such as the great pyramids and the Sphinx.

The Israelites sometimes called Egypt "Mizraim". God's people respected and feared the Egyptians. Several times, Egypt was a place of safety for the people of Israel. When Jacob's son Joseph came to Egypt, he was eventually able to save the lives of his whole family through his work there. And when Jesus was born, Mary's husband Joseph took the family to Egypt to escape from King Herod.

Frequently Asked Questions

Q: Who were some of the other prophets to Israel at this time?
A: Jeremiah, Daniel, and Habakkuk were prophets of God at the same time as Ezekiel. He was not alone. Sometimes it may seem believers are alone, but God always has people who love and obey him.

Q: Why was God so angry with the Israelites?
A: God's people were behaving as badly as the other peoples around them. They were praying to idols, sacrificing their children to false gods, robbing the poor and murdering – completely turning their backs on God.

Study Question

- What did God want the people of Israel to do? (18:30–32)

One of the huge human-headed bulls that guarded the entrance to the throne room of the royal palace at Nineveh, Babylon.

DANIEL

Daniel at peace in the lions' pit.

OUTLINE

Stories of Daniel's life (1–6)
Daniel and his friends gain the king's trust. Daniel becomes known as a wise man. His friends are saved from the fiery furnace, and Daniel is saved from the lions' den.

Prophecy of the future (7–8)
Daniel has visions of a ram, a goat, and four beasts.

Prophecy of the coming Messiah (9)
Daniel prays for his people and prophesies about Jesus.

Prophecy of the end times (10–12)
Daniel describes visions and details about the end of the world.

Imagine being captured and taken to a foreign country. Imagine having your name changed and being given strange food to eat. Imagine seeing idols all around and people praying to them. That is what happened to Daniel and his three friends Shadrach, Meshach, and Abednego.

They were all young nobles from Jerusalem. Nebuchadnezzar wanted them to be trained to serve him. The book of Daniel records how these young men trusted God even in a strange land.

The book of Daniel shows how God was in control even when it seemed as if the king of Babylon was in control. God gave Daniel wisdom to know what the king had dreamed and how to interpret the dream. God also helped Shadrach, Meshach, and Abednego to bravely say no when the king demanded that they worship an idol. God did a miracle and saved them all. The book of Daniel shows that God was in control and had different jobs for each of them.

The second half of the book of Daniel is filled with prophecies about the future. These also show that God is in control.

A modern reconstruction of the Ishtar Gate, Babylon, Iraq.

Frequently Asked Questions

Q: Why were Daniel and his friends chosen to be trained for the king?
A: These young noblemen were handsome, intelligent, quick learners, and in excellent health. They were the kind of people the king wanted around him.

Q: Why did Nebuchadnezzar have Daniel and his friends' names changed?
A: Their Hebrew names gave praise to the Lord. Their Babylonian names referred to Babylonian gods. Nebuchadnezzar may have been trying to make them worship the Babylonian gods.

Q: What did Daniel do every day that got him thrown into the lions' den?
A: Daniel prayed three times every day. The king's officials knew this and tricked the king into making an unchangeable law. The law said no one could ask for anything from anyone except the king for thirty days. But Daniel continued his daily prayers to God.

A Babylonian warrior.

Look out for...

As you read through Daniel, look out for...

Decisions. *Daniel decides when he is young that he is going to live the kind of life God wants him to live. Each time he makes a decision, it's a decision to follow God's way of doing things.*

Prophecy. *Daniel explains the king's dreams and tells him about the future. Daniel also describes things that will happen in our future.*

Kings. *The book of Daniel mentions several different kings. This is because while Babylon is holding the Israelites captive, the nation keeps getting a new king.*

Study Question

- What decree did King Darius make when he saw that God had protected Daniel from the hungry lions? (6:25–27)

Furnace

The furnace that Daniel's friends were thrown into was not meant for people. It was the kind of furnace used for other purposes. At that time furnaces were used for smelting metals such as copper, tin, iron, and lead. Some were also used for making bricks and pottery. These furnaces were sometimes called "kilns". Other kinds of furnaces were used for baking bread. Sometimes the word for "furnace" was also translated as "oven".

The Persians had the idea of using this hot, fiery place for executions. Many furnaces had a hole at the top to throw in materials and a door at the bottom on the side to pull out the metals, bricks, or bread. The fire was especially hot in the furnace the day Daniel's friends were thrown in. Even the guards were burnt to death when they came near. It was truly a miracle that God could protect the men inside the fiery furnace.

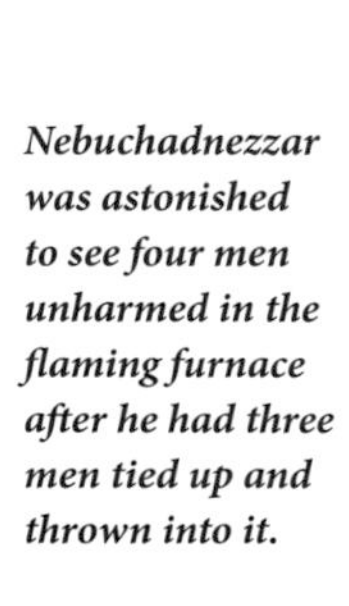

Nebuchadnezzar was astonished to see four men unharmed in the flaming furnace after he had three men tied up and thrown into it.

HOSEA

OUTLINE

Hosea's unhappy marriage (1–3)

Even though Hosea's wife is unfaithful to him, he continues to take care of her.

Israel's sin (4–7)

Hosea describes the sin of Israel, accusing them of praying to other gods and not trusting the one true God to take care of them.

God will judge them soon (8–10)

Israel will be punished for disobeying God.

God is faithful (11–14)

Hosea reminds the people of Israel that God loves them and is kind to those who love him in return.

Look out for...

As you read through Hosea, look out for...

Meanings of names. *Hosea chooses the names of his children for a reason. Notice what these names mean.*

Israel and Judah. *When Hosea was prophesying, the Jewish kingdom was divided into Judah and Israel. Hosea addressed them together at times and separately at other times.*

God's love. *The book of Hosea includes beautiful words of love from God to his people.*

It's very sad when husbands and wives get divorced. In the book of Hosea, God compares Israel (the northern kingdom) to a wife. He tells Israel that he loves her and wants her to stay. But she is interested in other men (that is, other gods).

The prophet Hosea went through the same sorrow that God was going through. Hosea married a woman named Gomer, but Gomer left him for other men. Even some of her children were fathered by other men. But God told Hosea to bring her home and keep on loving her. Hosea's love for Gomer was like God's love for his people.

The people of Israel were unfaithful to God. They put their trust in military help from Assyria and Egypt. They followed the false god Baal and mixed idol-worship with worship of the Lord. They were rich, but disloyal to God. It broke God's heart. God sent Hosea to urge the people to come back to him.

Like Ezekiel, Hosea often acted out his prophecies. Here he has a bag of silver and ten bushels of grain (see chapter 3).

Jezreel

Jezreel is a city on the border of the land given to the tribe of Issachar. The first son of Hosea and Gomer was named after this city.

The evil king Ahab built his palace in Jezreel (see pages 54–55). It was there that Ahab had a man named Naboth killed so that Ahab could get his vineyard. It was there that Ahab met Elijah and that evil Queen Jezebel met her death. From this city there was an excellent view of a plain called the Valley of Jezreel.

Study Questions

- What did Hosea say when he asked Israel to repent? (14:1–3)
- What did God promise to do if the people repented? (14:4–8)

Frequently Asked Questions

Q: Why did God tell Hosea to marry an unfaithful wife?

A: God wanted his people to see his love as they watched Hosea. The people could see how unfaithful Gomer was, and how much Hosea loved her. They didn't understand that they were unfaithful to God, just like Gomer was to Hosea. Hosea and Gomer were an "object lesson" for God's people.

Q: What kind of things were the people of Israel doing that made God punish them?

A: The people forgot God and his ways. They were turning to idols. They were lying, stealing, cursing, murdering, committing adultery, and doing all kinds of violence right across the land.

JOEL

OUTLINE

The locust plague (1:1 – 2:18)

Joel predicts a plague of locusts (grasshoppers) and an invasion by the enemy.

God will bless and judge (2:19 – 3:21)

Joel predicts the end of the world, when God will redeem his people and restore Israel.

Look out for...

As you read through Joel, look out for...

Plague. *God often uses extreme natural events to get the attention of his people.*

End times. *Joel describes many things that will happen when Jesus comes back to rule the world.*

How many locusts would it take to block out the sun like a dark rain-cloud? That's how many locusts the prophet Joel predicted would attack the crops of Judah. In the book of Joel, the prophet tried to arouse the people of Judah from their sin.

He told them that God was going to send such a huge plague of locusts that nothing would remain. Every bit of vegetation would be eaten by the insects. No food would be left.

Some people wonder if Joel was speaking of actual locusts. They think he might have been talking about a mighty army that would destroy everything. Whatever he meant, the destruction would be terrible. Joel urged the southern kingdom of Judah to repent and turn back to God.

Judah was prosperous at the time of Joel. But instead of thanking God, the people turned to idol-worship and sin. They thought everything was just fine.

Joel warned of "the day of the Lord", a time still in the future when God will judge everyone and put everything right. But even though God is the all-powerful judge, he is still merciful. He wants people to repent and turn to him. He wants to bless those who trust him.

Joel warns about the coming day of the Lord.

Locusts

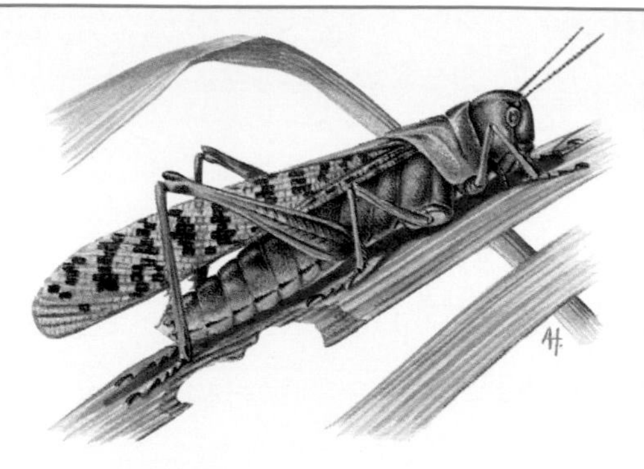

Locusts are a kind of grasshopper. They fly in swarms and can destroy large amounts of crops or green plants in a short amount of time. In the Bible, locusts are also referred to as "devourers", "pests", and "katydids". While locusts can eat a lot, they are also eaten themselves, as in Leviticus 11:21–22. John the Baptist ate locusts and wild honey (Mark 1:6).

God used locusts as a punishment once before. When Moses was freeing the Israelites from Egypt, one of the ten plagues was a plague of locusts (Exodus 10:4–15). The prophet Joel describes a terrifying plague of locusts that would come to punish Israel's sin (1:2–4). These descriptions are nothing compared with the prediction in Revelation 9:3–10. The locusts there are described as a great army with the ability to destroy everything in their path.

Study Questions

- What was the army of locusts like? (2:1–11)
- What promise did the Lord give to everyone? (2:32)

Frequently Asked Questions

Q: Why did Joel talk about locusts?
A: Locusts travel in swarms and eat all the plants and crops in their path. They can completely wipe out an entire field of crops in hours. Joel said that when God judged, it would be like a storm of locusts. This would scare anyone who knew how destructive a locust swarm could be. God wanted this message to shock the people into listening to him!

Q: What does it mean to "turn to God"?
A: Turning to God does not mean just going to church or believing that God exists. God wants people to be sorry for their sin and to stop doing it. He wants people to ask his forgiveness. Spending time talking with him and reading his Word to learn his will is important.

AMOS

OUTLINE

God judges foreign nations (1–2)

God calls Amos and announces that Israel will be punished for its sin and corruption.

God judges Samaria (3–6)

Amos makes several prophecies, each beginning with a call for the people to listen.

Warnings – and a promise (7–9)

Five visions (bad news) and some closing promises (good news).

A farmer speaking to city people might feel worried about telling them about their sin – but not Amos. Amos was a shepherd from the southern kingdom. God sent him to warn the Israelites in the northern kingdom. The book of Amos is the record of Amos's message.

Amos started out warning the surrounding nations about their constant wrongdoing. Then he spoke against the people of Judah. Perhaps the people of Israel cheered him on. But then he spoke against Israel too. He said that everyone would have to answer to God.

Amaziah the high priest opposed Amos and reported him to King Jeroboam II. As you might expect, Amos's message was not popular. Amos spoke against the Israelites because of their attitude. They were wealthy and happy. That's all that mattered to them. They neglected the poor. They sold them into slavery to buy luxuries for themselves.

The Israelites made a show of religion. But they prayed to idols and didn't follow God. Amos told them to repent.

About twenty-eight years after Amos finished speaking to Israel, God kept his promise. Wealthy Israelites who sold their countrymen into slavery became slaves themselves. The Assyrians took them away to other lands.

God showed Amos a basket of ripe fruit, warning him: "This is the end for my people Israel..." (8:1–2, CEV)

Assyrian relief picturing warriors in battle.

Frequently Asked Questions

Q: Why did the nations around Israel deserve God's punishment?
A: They had mistreated God's people. Even though the people of Israel and Judah forgot God and sinned against him, they were still God's chosen people.

Q: What was Amos's message to Israel?
A: Amos reminded the people of Israel about all that God had done to grab their attention. God sent disaster and drought, and sent mildew on their gardens to get them to recognize his power. Instead, they boasted about their wealth and did not trust God.

Q: What bad things did the Israelites do?
A: They took bribes. They sold the poor into slavery. They pretended to worship God. They boasted about giving offerings to God. They cared more about things than about God or other people.

Plumb line

A plumb line is a cord or a string with a weight tied to the end. (It's also called a "plummet".) Plumb lines were used by masons and builders. They would hang up the string and let the weight at the bottom pull down on it. They would then use the string as a guide, to help them build an upright wall.

The plumb line was also used to inspect a wall to see if it had been well built. This use is described in the vision in Amos 7:7–9. God said that he would hold up a plumb line to Israel. He explained that this plumb line would measure righteousness. It would reveal the sin, which he would then correct.

Look out for...

As you read through Amos, look out for...

Messages from God. *More than once Amos says, "Listen to what the Lord says..."*

Visions. *Amos's visions include fire, a plumb line, ripe fruit, and God at an altar.*

Study Question

- What does God promise Israel? (9:11–15)

OBADIAH

OUTLINE

God judges Edom (1:1–16)
Through Obadiah's vision, God judges Edom for causing harm to Israel and rejoicing in that harm.

Israel will be restored (1:17–21)
Obadiah describes a time when Israel will have great power over Edom.

Look out for…

As you read through Obadiah, look out for…

Reasons for God's judgment. *Obadiah lists some things for which God holds Edom responsible.*

Signs of Israel's restoration. *God describes the shift in power when Israel gets the upper hand over Edom.*

Brothers should help one other, especially when one is being beaten up by a bully. But the people of Edom did not help their brothers, the Israelites.

The people of Edom were related to the people of Israel. They both had Abraham and Isaac as their ancestors. The Edomites were descendants of Esau. The Israelites were descended from Esau's brother, Jacob.

The book of Obadiah tells of God's punishment for the people of Edom. They did not help their Israelite relatives in Judah. When the Babylonians attacked Jerusalem, the Edomites cheered them on. They actually helped the Babylonians capture the people of Judah! Then they plundered Jerusalem and took what had been left behind. The Edomites were proud and thought nothing could hurt them.

Obadiah is the shortest book in the Old Testament, but gives an important message. God takes care of his people and punishes those who hurt them.

Obadiah warned that the people of Edom were doomed.

The Treasury building in the Edomite city of Petra, in modern Jordan, is cut out of the natural rock face.

Edom

The people of Edom were descended from Esau. Their country was also called Seir, or Mount Seir, situated between the Dead Sea and the Gulf of Aqabah. It was about 140 kilometres (87 miles) long and 25 kilometres (16 miles) wide.

When Esau came to this land he married the daughter of one of the Horites, or cave dwellers, who were already living there. As Esau's descendants grew, they eventually took over the land from the Horites. At one time, King David conquered the Edomites and had control of the whole country. During the reign of later kings, Edom won its independence again.

Esau and his twin brother Jacob (whose descendants are the Israelites) were often enemies of each other. No wonder their descendants mistreated each other and needed God to intervene.

Study Question

- What prophecy did Obadiah make about Israel and Edom? (1:17–18)

Frequently Asked Questions

Q: Where did the Edomites live?
A: The Edomites lived south of Judah. They shared a boundary with Judah and were close enough to help the people of Judah.

Q: Why were the Edomites so proud?
A: The people of Edom had carved a city out of the rocks. They lived high up in a fortress that seemed secure. They were very proud of themselves and thought they were safe.

Q: How did God judge Edom?
A: The nation of Edom was completely destroyed.

JONAH

A reconstruction of one of the gates of the ancient city of Nineveh.

The Hebrew people had a hard time learning that God wanted them to obey him. But after they had learned that lesson, they found it difficult to understand that God still loved people of other nations. The book of Jonah tells about Jonah's problem understanding that God loves everyone.

This is the only book of prophecy that tells more about the prophet than about the prophet's message.

Jonah was the first Jewish prophet sent on a mission to a non-Jewish country. He was a prophet to the northern kingdom of Israel. Then God sent him to Nineveh, the capital of the great Assyrian Empire.

The Assyrians were not nice people. They were fierce and cruel warriors. When God told Jonah to go to Nineveh to preach to its people, Jonah went off in the opposite direction.

Jonah tried to get as far away as possible. But even in a ship in the middle of the Mediterranean Sea, Jonah could not hide from God. After suffering for disobeying God, Jonah repented and obeyed the God's instructions.

Jonah learned that God's salvation is for all who repent and believe.

A Phoenician vessel, possibly similar to the boat Jonah boarded at Joppa to take him across the Mediterranean Sea.

OUTLINE

Jonah's call and escape (1)

God asks Jonah to go to Nineveh, but Jonah runs off the opposite way. During a storm, Jonah is thrown overboard from a boat and rescued by a large fish.

Jonah's prayer (2)

Jonah thanks and praises God for saving him, and the fish spits Jonah out onto the shore.

Preaching to Nineveh (3)

Jonah obeys God and preaches to the people of Nineveh.

Jonah is disappointed (4)

The people of Nineveh repent, and Jonah is disappointed that God doesn't punish them for their sins.

Frequently Asked Questions

Q: Why didn't Jonah want to preach to the people of Nineveh?

A: The people of Nineveh were enemies of Israel and very cruel. Jonah hated them. Jonah also knew that God is merciful and kind. He didn't want the people of Nineveh to repent because he knew God would forgive them if they did. Jonah wanted them to be punished for their wickedness.

Q: How did Jonah get swallowed by a fish?

A: God sent the fish to rescue Jonah from drowning in the sea. In fact, he sent the fish in answer to Jonah's prayer for help. The fish took Jonah to shore from the middle of the sea.

Nineveh

Nineveh was one of the most ancient cities of the world. It was founded on the banks of the River Tigris by Nimrod, Noah's great-grandson. For many years it was capital of the Assyrian Empire and was an important city from the time of King David until the reign of Manasseh.

Nineveh was ruled by kings except for about fifty years around 800 BC; probably when Jonah went to Nineveh and saw the people there repent of their sin.

Nineveh was destroyed by the Assyrians around 612 BC, just after Nahum prophesied against the city.

Look out for...

As you read through Jonah, look out for...

Jonah's pride. *It shows up more than once.*

Jonah's prayers. *In his prayers, Jonah is honest with God, even when he is angry.*

Study Questions

- What was it like for Jonah in the sea and inside the fish? (2:1–9)
- What happened when Jonah preached to the people of Nineveh? (3:1–10)
- Why did Jonah become angry? (4:1–4)

MICAH

It's not enough for people to worship God but forget what God teaches them. God expects people who love him to be kind and merciful to others. He wants them to do good. And he wants them to worship him sincerely.

The prophet Micah explained this in the book of Micah. He said God would judge Samaria (in Israel) and Jerusalem (in Judah) for disobeying God. But he also told them that the Messiah would bring hope and peace.

Hundreds of years before Jesus was born, Micah predicted that the Messiah would be born in Bethlehem. It was this prediction that the wise men followed. They asked King Herod in Jerusalem where the new king was. The priests told them he was in Bethlehem.

Micah was a prophet at the same time as Isaiah and Hosea. His book is written in Hebrew poetry. He condemned those who stole, lied, oppressed the poor, murdered, craved money, and pretended to worship God.

While Micah was a prophet, Assyria overran Israel. Micah predicted that Judah would fall too. But the Messiah would be the new king – a righteous, good king.

The prophet Micah wrote in poetry rather than prose.

OUTLINE

Lying prophets (1–3)

Micah speaks directly to Samaria and Jerusalem (the two Jewish capitals) about the sin of the people and of the leaders.

Christ's coming kingdom (4–5)

Micah predicts Jesus' birth and never-ending reign.

God judges and forgives (6–7)

Micah sets out God's case against Israel, and Israel's hope of God's forgiveness.

Look out for...

As you read through Micah, look out for...

The Messiah. *Micah tells about Jesus' coming long before it happens. He even names the town where Jesus will be born.*

Advice. *Micah gives good advice on how to follow God in our everyday lives.*

Samaria. *Micah talks a lot about the punishment the people of Samaria will receive for their sins.*

Samaria

"Samaria" can mean a city, a region or a country. When the Israelite kingdom split into the northern and southern kingdoms, the northern kingdom built the city of Samaria as its capital. The land where they built the city was bought from a man named Shemer, and it's from this word that the city got its name.

The northern kingdom was made up of ten tribes of Israelites. Sometimes people refer to Samaria as all the land held by those ten tribes.

Micah prophesied to both the city of Samaria (capital of the northern kingdom) and the city of Jerusalem (capital of the southern kingdom). Both cities were full of Israelites who had disobeyed and forgotten the one true God.

Samaria was built on a hill. It had a wall all the way around it (like most cities at that time) and gates that could be closed at night and during an attack. Samaria stood through many battles, and its ruins are still there today.

A view of the site of the city of Samaria today.

Frequently Asked Questions

Q: Why would God punish Israel and Judah?

A: The people were ignoring God's instructions to treat each other with respect. They were taking property from widows and other poor people. False prophets were saying everything was fine. God wanted them to know that these matters were important.

Q: But if God loves his people, how could he hurt them?

A: It is because God loves people that he punishes sin. He wants people to repent and turn to him. Sometimes when people are enjoying God's blessings, they forget him. He has to get their attention. Sometimes he does that by punishing them.

Q: How were the priests pretending to worship God?

A: The priests carried out the correct ceremonies. But in their hearts they were scheming to get money and power.

Study Questions

- What prophecy of Micah's came true in Bethlehem? (5:2–5; Matthew 2:1–6)
- How does Micah describe God? (7:18–20)

NAHUM

An Assyrian army attacks an Israelite city. Assyrian soldiers were greatly feared in the ancient world. They captured many towns and cities of Israel and Judah.

Some nations are so powerful that it seems as if they can never be defeated. That's how it was with Assyria. Assyria had a huge, powerful, fierce army.

They had strong chariots with sharp knives sticking out of their wheel hubs. The soldiers were not afraid of anyone. They killed more people than could be counted. They plundered nation after nation. They had no sense of right and wrong. Being cruel to their prisoners didn't worry them.

When Jonah preached to them, they had repented. But by the time Nahum became a prophet, about a hundred years later, they were just as wicked as before.

Nahum's book is God's message to Nineveh, the great capital of Assyria. The news was not good. God had run out of patience with Nineveh.

An Assyrian warrior.

OUTLINE

God's nature (1)

God's anger, patience, and power.

Nineveh's destruction (2–3)

Nahum describes the destruction of Nineveh and God's reasons for destroying it.

The Assyrians had taken Israel captive. Now God, the righteous Judge, was going to destroy wicked Assyria. Nothing could be worse than to have God against you!

But there is also good news in the book of Nahum. God promised the people of Judah that Assyria would never again harm Judah.

Assyria

Assyria was right beside Babylonia. They fought all the time and moved their border back and forth. Israel was next to both of these empires, and often had to fight them. Israel was taken over by both empires for a time.

Assyria was probably started by a colony of Babylonians, so their culture and religion were similar. The Assyrians regarded the false god Asshur as their founder. Their other gods included Anu, Bel, Ea, Shamash, and Ishtar. While the Assyrians fought the Babylonians, at times they worked together and almost gained control of the whole region. Assyria's capital was Nineveh.

Assyrian relief depicting an archer and an infantryman.

Look out for...

As you read through Nahum, look out for...

God's nature. *Even though this is a prophecy against Assyria, this book tells us a lot about God.*

Punishment. *Nahum makes it clear that the people of Assyria will be punished severely for their sin.*

Study Question

- Why do some people say God is angry all the time, while others say he is loving? (1:7–8)

Frequently Asked Questions

Q: How did God destroy Assyria?

A: God used other nations to destroy Assyria. In 612 BC he used the Babylonians and the Medes to fight Assyria. They did to Assyria what it had done so many times to other nations. They waged war against the people and took all its wealth. The city of Nineveh was so completely destroyed that no one could identify its ruins until 1845 – more than 2,000 years later!

HABAKKUK

A mythical creature depicted in glazed tiles from a wall in ancient Babylon.

It's not much fun watching the news or reading the newspaper these days. People steal, lie, cheat, beat up others, kill their enemies – and their friends – and do many other wicked things. Believe it or not, this is no different from when the prophet Habakkuk lived in Judah more than 2,500 years ago!

Habakkuk had the same questions that many people have today. He asked God why he wasn't doing anything about all this evil. Habakkuk knew God is just and holy. He couldn't understand how God could let the bad people get away with doing bad things.

Habakkuk did the right thing with his questions. He went to God with them. God answered him and gave him a message that people can still read today.

God had a plan that was stranger than anything Habakkuk could imagine! God was going to use the Babylonians to punish the people of Judah.

OUTLINE

Habakkuk's problem (1–2)

Habakkuk asks questions, and God gives his replies.

Habakkuk's prayer (3)

Habakkuk sees that God is great and sings this prayer to praise him.

This created more questions for Habakkuk. The Babylonians were far more wicked than the people of Judah. How could God use them to punish his people? The Babylonians were proud. They didn't know God was using them to turn his people back to him. The Babylonians' sins would be their undoing.

God assured Habakkuk that one day he would punish all those who are against God. But those who trust in God will have true life (2:4).

Babylonia

Babylonia was a powerful kingdom known for many things, especially two famous cities. The capital city of Babylonia was Babylon, mentioned in both the New and Old Testaments. Another important Babylonian city was Ur, where Abraham came from.

Babylonia is famous for its unique style of pottery, the beginnings of writing called "cuneiform", the oldest ziggurat or tall tower at that time, and a special style of weaving (see Joshua 7:21). Because the country was so large and so close to the Jewish nation, it was always a threat. Countries at that time were forever trying to widen their borders and take over other countries.

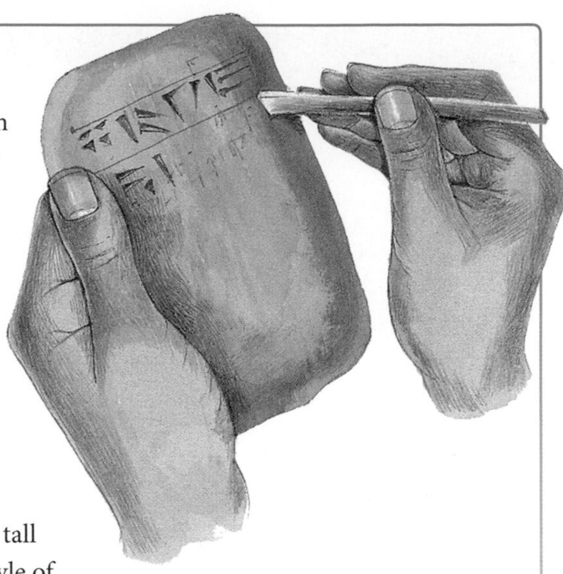

Cuneiform writing was done using a wedge-shaped stylus in damp clay. The clay was later hardened into a tablet to preserve the message.

Look out for...

As you read through Habakkuk, look out for...

***Questions.** Habakkuk asks God some hard questions.*

***Answers.** God answers Habakkuk's questions.*

***Praises.** Habakkuk praises God for his greatness.*

Study Questions

- What promises did God give to Habakkuk? (2:14, 20)
- How did Habakkuk praise God? (3:1–19)
- What did Habakkuk promise God? (3:17–18)

Frequently Asked Questions

Q: What did God do when Habakkuk asked hard questions?
A: God didn't get angry with Habakkuk. He answered his questions and explained that justice would be done. God said there was a set time for this, and told Habakkuk to be patient and wait for it.

Q: What did Habakkuk do with God's answers?
A: At first Habakkuk was even more confused. Then he saw that God is in control. He asked God to have mercy on Judah when the time of discipline came. Then he praised God.

ZEPHANIAH

OUTLINE

God will judge Judah soon (1 – 2:3)

Zephaniah tells that soon Jerusalem will be destroyed.

God will judge all nations (2:4–15)

Zephaniah tells about the time when God will judge the whole world.

Jerusalem rebels and is redeemed (3)

God will one day purify his people.

God had sent many prophets to warn the people of Judah that he would judge them soon. The book of Zephaniah was one of the last written before the Jews were exiled to Babylonia.

Zephaniah prophesied during the reign of King Josiah of Judah. He also prophesied when Jeremiah started giving God's messages to the people of Jerusalem. King Josiah was the last good king of Judah. He worked hard to lead the people away from idols and back to God. Zephaniah probably helped Josiah to understand God's Word and to apply it to his people.

Manasseh and Amon, two kings before Josiah, had led the people far from God. They had turned to idols such as Baal, Molech, and others. Molech-worship included sacrificing children! God hated this. The people thought they could worship both the true God and idols.

The "day of the Lord" that Zephaniah predicted had two meanings: first, the Babylonian Exile; second, the last days. At that time, God will punish all who have rejected him. Those who trust in him will live with him in heaven.

Prisoners from Judah are marched into exile by the cruel Babylonians.

Relief of the Canaanite deity Baal.

Moab and Ammon

The countries of Moab and Ammon were named after the families (tribes) that settled there. The families were named after their most important ancestor.

Lot was Abraham's nephew. He got involved with two very sinful cities, Sodom and Gomorrah. After he left those cities, each of his daughters had a son. The names of these sons were Moab and Ammon. When Moab and Ammon grew up they moved away, and their families settled in these lands that were then named after them. After many years, the people of Israel (Abraham's descendants) came back to settle their land, and the people of Moab and Ammon (descendants of Moab and Ammon) fought against them.

Zephaniah prophesied against Moab and Ammon because they fought against Israel, because they tried to take land that was not theirs, and because they tried to get Israel to be unfaithful to God.

The barren hills of Moab, with the Dead Sea in the distance.

Frequently Asked Questions

Q: If Josiah and Zephaniah helped the people turn back to God, why did God still punish them?

A: Josiah truly wanted to please God, but most of his people did not have a real change of heart. A few years after Josiah died, the people continued their sinful ways.

Q: How can Zephaniah's prophecy have two meanings?

A: Actually, several prophecies in the Old Testament work in this way. The first meaning came about soon after the prophet had spoken. The second meaning would come about later. Some of Zephaniah's prophecies tell of events still in the future.

Look out for...

As you read through Zephaniah, look out for...

Day of the Lord. *Zephaniah talks about two Days of the Lord. These are days when God intervenes in the world in a big way. One of those days will be at the end of the world as we know it.*

Joy. *Even though Zephaniah is talking about punishment, there is a lot of joy at the end of his message.*

Study Question

- What good promise did God make to Israel? (3:14–20)

HAGGAI

Soon after King Cyrus defeated the Babylonians, he let the Jews return to Jerusalem to rebuild the Temple. The returned exiles started this task, but enemies threatened and discouraged them. For as long as ten years they stopped work on the Temple. God sent the prophet Haggai to get the people to finish the job.

Haggai's messages are recorded in the book of Haggai. Haggai and Zechariah worked with Ezra and Nehemiah to help the Jews.

The Jewish people were busy building their own homes, but left God's Temple in ruins. Haggai said this wasn't right. He reminded them that they needed to finish the Temple. They were working hard but had little to show for it. Haggai said this was because God was working against them.

OUTLINE

Rebuilding the Temple (1:1 – 2:9)

Haggai encourages the people to rebuild the Temple now and stop putting it off.

Promises (2:10–23)

God promises to meet the people's needs if they will finish their work on the Temple.

Haggai said the people should put first things first: they should rebuild God's Temple. They should care about spiritual matters; then God would satisfy their needs and their hearts.

Haggai reminded the Jews that it was important to rebuild God's Temple as well as their own homes.

View of the Old City of Jerusalem, Israel, and the Temple Mount from the Mount of Olives.

The Temple

Solomon built the first Temple with the finest building materials. But each time the Israelites turned away from God, they stopped taking care of it. And each time enemies fought them, those enemies would try to destroy it. This is why, in the Old Testament, we often read about the Temple being rebuilt.

During the time of Haggai, the Temple had been completely destroyed. The Israelites did not have much money or many resources to build a beautiful Temple again. But they tried. Zerubbabel was the governor in charge of the city. Joshua (not the Joshua who succeeded Moses) was their religious ruler. Together they led the people to rebuild the Temple. It was not as fine as Solomon's Temple, but it reminded the people that it was important to worship God.

Frequently Asked Questions

Q: What were the people doing in Jerusalem all those years?
A: They settled down to live and to build their own homes. Some lived in expensive houses. They grew lots of grain, grapes, and olive trees. But they weren't building the Temple.

Q: What did the people do after Haggai spoke to them?
A: The leaders and the people quickly followed Haggai's advice. Within weeks they got on with rebuilding the Temple.

Q: After the people obeyed him, what did God do?
A: As soon as the people started work on the Temple, God said he would bless them and make their crops grow.

Look out for...

As you read through Haggai, look out for...

Dates. *This book gives us the dates of Haggai's messages.*

Inspiration. *Haggai was like a cheerleader, encouraging God's people to work on the Temple.*

Results. *The people responded to Haggai and rebuilt the Temple.*

Study Questions

- How did God encourage his people? (2:4–5)
- What did God say to the people as soon as they started work? (2:18–19)

ZECHARIAH

What would it be like to know the future? God gave the prophets messages about the future. Some of these messages were warnings that God would judge the people if they didn't repent of sin and turn to him. Some messages gave hope of comfort and peace.

Zechariah was a prophet who had returned from exile to Jerusalem. He worked with the prophet Haggai to encourage the people to continue building the Temple. His message told of God's anger and his love.

Of all the Old Testament books, the book of Zechariah is filled with the most prophecies about the Messiah. There are prophecies about his first coming to earth, when he was crucified and rose again. There are prophecies about his second coming as King. There are many prophecies about the end of time.

People who read and study God's Word today can know a little of what the future holds. God doesn't give us exact dates, but he warns us not to follow false prophets. He promises that, at the end of time, those who reject God will be punished forever. Those who trust Jesus Christ the Messiah will enjoy his peace and everlasting life.

OUTLINE

Introduction and visions (1–6)

Zechariah tells about visions of horns, blacksmiths, olive trees, lampstands, and flying scrolls.

True worship (7–8)

Zechariah encourages his people to trust God and to repair the Temple.

The future of Israel (9–14)

Zechariah predicts that God will judge Israel's enemies, protect Israel, and rule the earth.

Like Haggai, the prophet Zechariah urged the people to trust God and rebuild the Temple.

Myrtle trees

In one of Zechariah's visions, he sees a man (who was really an angel) standing among some myrtle trees. A myrtle is a small evergreen shrub with white flowers, blue berries, and scented leaves. The Jews thought that this plant stood for peace and prosperity. When the Jews celebrated their Festival of Shelters (or "tabernacles") they used myrtle branches to cover the shelters they lived in.

Zechariah thought of myrtle as a plant of peace. It must have been comforting for Zechariah to get good news from an angel who was surrounded by myrtles.

***An Orthodox Jew holding myrtle twigs, together with other plants associated with the Festival of Shelters, or* Sukkot.**

Look out for…

As you read through Zechariah, look out for…

***Visions.** Zechariah has eight visions or dreams.*

***Prophecies.** Zechariah makes many prophecies that came true in the life of Jesus.*

Study Questions

- What instructions did God give the people? (8:16–17)
- How does Zechariah's prophecy about the king compare with Jesus' enactment of the prophecy? (9:9–10; Matthew 21:1–11)

Frequently Asked Questions

Q: How do we know that Jesus is the Messiah that Zechariah was talking about?

A: Zechariah wrote his prophecies about 500 years before Jesus was born. Jesus' life matches many details given in Zechariah's prophecies. Jesus is the only one who fits the description Zechariah gave.

Q: What's so great about Jesus matching these prophecies?

A: Since God's Word is true concerning Jesus' first coming to earth, we can be confident that his other promises are true too. God warns that he is going to judge people and promises blessings for those who love him.

MALACHI

Malachi was the last of the prophets to Judah and Israel. The Temple had been rebuilt. The walls of Jerusalem had been completed. But the people were cutting corners in their worship of God.

The priests were not doing the sacrifices properly. Men were divorcing their wives and marrying younger women who prayed to idols. Children were growing up believing in idols. And the people weren't tithing (giving one tenth of) their crops and animals to God. This was a lot like stealing from God.

Malachi made it clear that God's people had to take their worship more seriously, and promised blessing for those who did. His very last words told of another prophet who would help the people before God judged them.

Malachi was the last of the prophets to Israel and Judah until Jesus came.

OUTLINE

Worthless worship (1:1 – 2:9)

God confronts Israel's leaders about their sin.

A call to repent (2:10–17)

Malachi reminds his people to trust God and be faithful to him.

God will judge people (3–4)

Malachi predicts that God will judge and purify people.

Model of first-century Jerusalem, showing the Temple Mount area (top left).

Grapes

Often in the Old Testament, when a prophet talks about a time when things are going well, he mentions grapes. Sometimes he says that grapes will bring much wine. Sometimes, as in Malachi, he says the grapes won't wither (dry up).

Grapes are one of the first plants mentioned in the Bible (Genesis 9:20). They grow on climbing vines that can either be left to grow wild or can be tended, or cultivated, in vineyards. For the Jews, grapes were a symbol of wealth and good fortune. The grape harvest (the time they picked the grapes) was a time of celebration and rejoicing.

Look out for...

As you read through Malachi, look out for...

Questions and answers. *Malachi uses questions and answers throughout his messages.*

Priests. *Much of what Malachi says about priests applies to church leaders today.*

Study Questions

- How did the people make God tired? (2:17)
- How will God treat those who trust him? (3:16–18)
- Who is the prophet like Elijah whom God promised? (4:5–6; Matthew 17:10–13)

Frequently Asked Questions

Q: **What was wrong with sacrificing a sick animal?**
A: God used sacrifices to show the seriousness of sin and the need for forgiveness. God is holy and requires our best – not something sick or broken.

Q: **How did the priests mess up worship?**
A: The priests weren't showing respect to God. They complained about making sacrifices. As leaders, they influenced people's attitudes and actions. Also, they weren't teaching the truth.

Q: **Why does God hate divorce?**
A: God wants husbands and wives to love each other and be faithful to each other. He knows that people, especially children, get hurt badly when families break up. He wants families to be safe and happy places for children to grow up in.

Cutaway illustration of a large peasant's house in New Testament times. Look for the women making bread, the bread oven, cooking pots, and indoor space for the animals.

The New Testament

The New Testament part of the Bible consists of twenty-seven different books. Nearly all these books were written in the first fifty years after the death and resurrection of Jesus. Like the Old Testament, they were written by various people in different circumstances and for different reasons. But also like the Old Testament, God's Spirit brought them all together to tell one story: the story of Jesus Christ.

The books that make up the New Testament are not placed in the order in which they were written. They are placed in order according to what type of book they are.

Gospels

The first four books are called Gospels: the Gospels of Matthew, Mark, Luke, and John. Each book is named after the man who wrote it. Each man told the story of Jesus: his ministry, death, and resurrection. Although each writer is talking about the same person, Jesus, they each remember different stories and different parts of the same stories, just as you would if you and your friend were both talking about an important person in your life. This is one thing that makes the Gospels so interesting.

The Gospels are followed by another book of history called Acts, or the Acts of the Apostles. This book begins where the Gospels end – after Jesus rose from the dead. It tells about the way the apostles chose a new disciple to take Judas's place. It tells the story of the thirty years after Jesus' life on earth. It tells how the church began and how Christianity spread. Acts was written by Luke, the same man who wrote the Gospel of Luke.

A city gate in New Testament times. Notice the Roman soldiers, the traders and beggars, and the various animals.

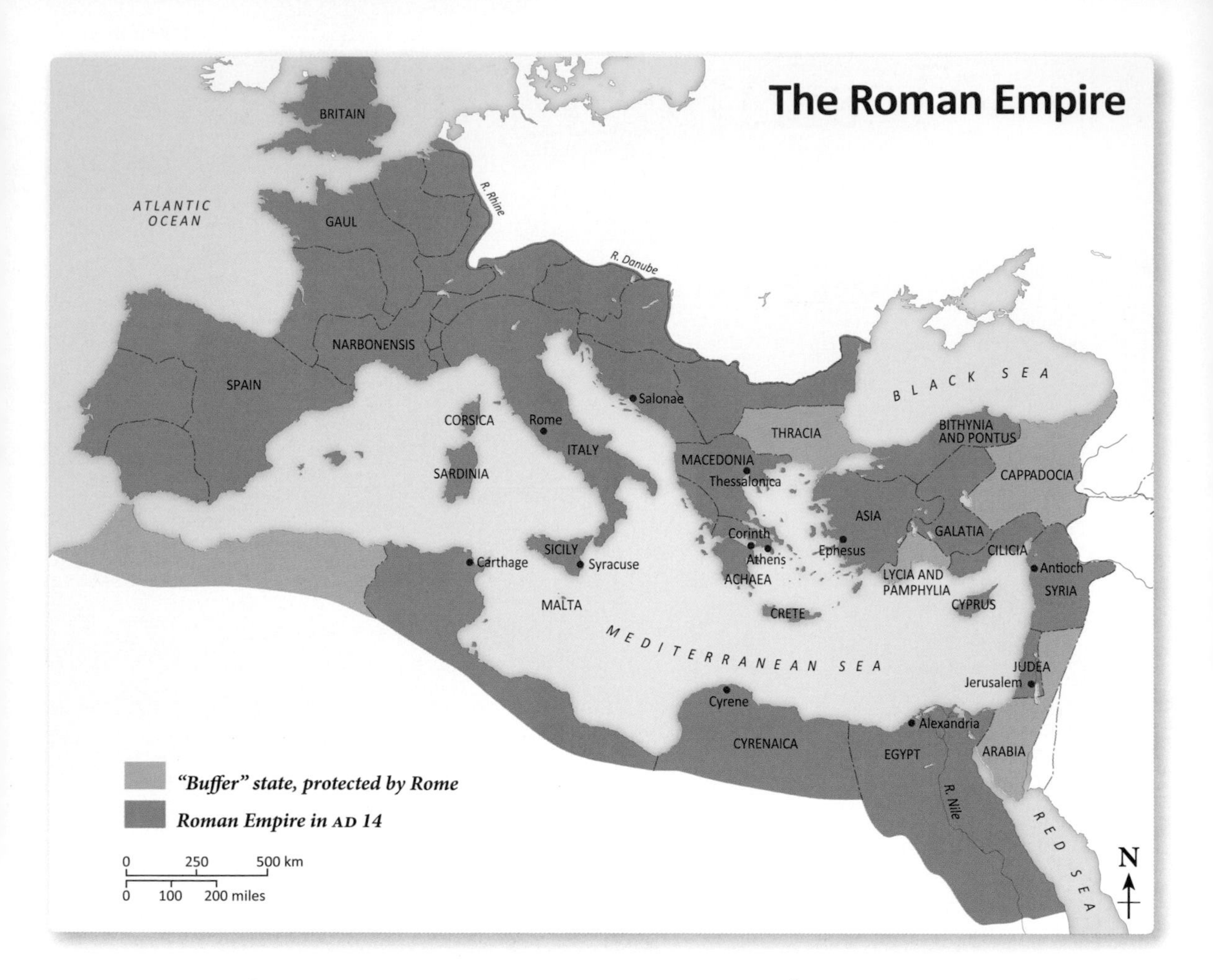

Letters

The next twenty-one books in the New Testament are letters or "epistles". Some are letters to people. Some are letters to churches or groups of believers. Thirteen were written by Paul, a famous apostle who came to know Jesus after Jesus' life on earth. Paul's letters are placed in order according to length, from the longest to the shortest. There are also three letters by John (who wrote the Gospel of John), two letters by Peter (a fisherman and disciple of Jesus), one by James, and one by Jude. We don't know who wrote Hebrews, but it was certainly someone who cared about obeying God and teaching his people.

Revelation

The last book of the New Testament is called Revelation. Revelation is an "apocalyptic" writing. That means it teaches about God's plan through word pictures and "visions" that God gave to the writer, John. This is the same John who wrote the Gospel of John.

The New Testament teaches us how Jesus lived and how we should live. It tells us about the difficult situations churches can get into and gives advice on how Christians should behave towards each other. The New Testament gives us hope that Jesus is coming again and that, one day, we will have a home with him in heaven.

New Testament Timeline

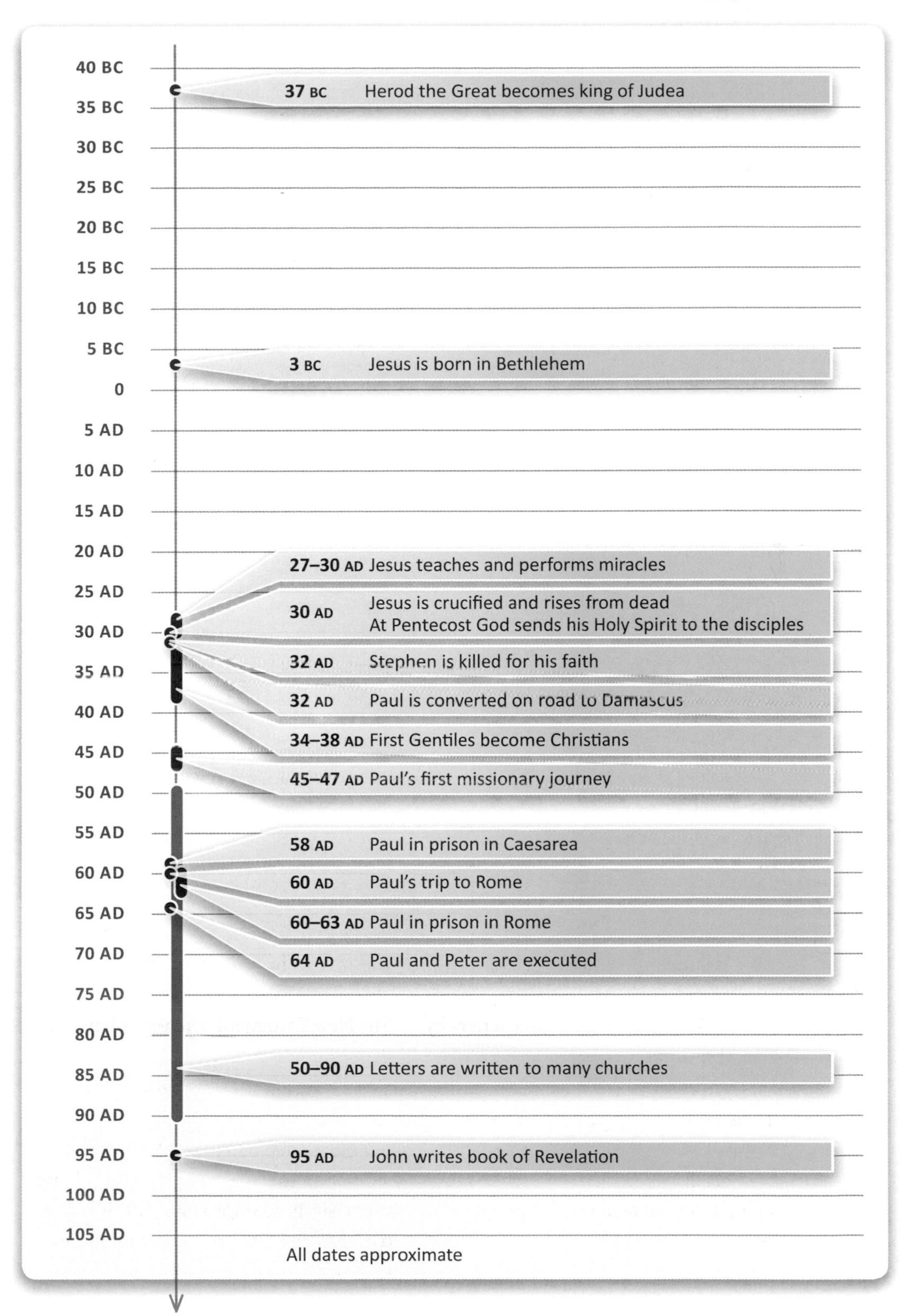

The Life and Times of Jesus

Jesus is the main person in the whole Bible. In the very first book of the Bible, God said someone would crush Satan. It was the first promise of salvation. All through the Old Testament, God's messengers, the prophets, tell of someone who would come to make things right.

The New Testament is all about that Messiah, Jesus Christ. It tells about his birth, life, teachings, miracles, death, and resurrection. It also tells about his followers and how they spread the Good News about Jesus.

The special baby

Jesus came into the world like no other child before him. A young Jewish woman named Mary was engaged to be married to a carpenter named Joseph. Mary was a virgin. Then God's Holy Spirit made Mary pregnant. Joseph was not the father – God was. Centuries before Jesus was born, God's messengers had said that was how it would happen. Jesus would be the Son of God and the Son of Man at the same time.

An angel told Mary she would have God's special baby. Later, an angel told Joseph that Mary was pregnant by the Spirit of God, and that Joseph should still marry her. And when Jesus was born, angels announced his birth to shepherds. God sent a special star to guide wise men to the new king of the Jews. Two old people who loved God, named Simeon and Anna, recognized the baby Jesus as the one whom God had promised long ago.

Joseph was a carpenter and Jesus learned his earthly father's trade. Joseph and Mary had other children who were Jesus' half-brothers and -sisters. They all lived in Nazareth. In most ways, their family was like any other ordinary Jewish family in Nazareth.

Shepherds come to visit the newborn baby Jesus in the stable in Bethlehem.

When Jesus was twelve years old, he went to Jerusalem with his parents for a special holiday called Passover. Later, Mary and Joseph found him talking with the religious teachers. Everyone was amazed at how much he understood and knew.

For many years Jesus worked as a carpenter. He probably seemed quite ordinary. But when he was about thirty years old, things changed.

Jesus and John

Jesus had a cousin named John. John was called the "Baptizer" or "Baptist" because he baptized people, dipping them in the river. John was preparing the way for the Messiah. When Jesus went to John to be baptized, John heard God say to Jesus, "You are my dearly loved Son, and you bring me great joy." (Luke 3:22)

After that, Jesus spent time in the desert where he prayed. He didn't eat anything for forty days. Satan tempted Jesus, trying to get Jesus to worship him and turn his back on God. But Jesus stood firm against the Devil. Jesus was ready to do the work that God had sent him to do.

The teacher

Jesus began teaching people about God. The religious leaders had made many extra rules about how to worship God. They had made it so hard for people to know God that many people just went through the motions of keeping the laws. Others gave up completely.

Many people liked listening to Jesus. Crowds followed him from town to town as he taught about God's love. Jesus always spent a lot of time praying to the Father. One day after praying, he chose twelve men to be his disciples. The men left their jobs. For three years they lived and journeyed with Jesus. They listened to his talks, watched his miracles, and asked questions about anything they didn't understand. He told them he was going to die and rise again. But they didn't understand everything he said until after Jesus' death and resurrection.

Jesus' cousin, John the Baptist, preached in the desert, calling on people to change their lives.

Jesus talked to the people in parables – stories he took from everyday life. He told them what God's kingdom is like. He said that his followers should love their enemies and serve each other. He taught about God's love for people. He talked about forgiveness, purity, faithfulness in marriage, honesty, keeping promises, obeying God, getting rid of sin, being thankful, and many other things.

The healer

Talking wasn't all that Jesus did. Jesus showed his love and power by healing people who were blind, unable to walk, unable to talk, and who had other serious

Jesus is arrested by the Temple guards in the Garden of Gethsemane.

diseases. He fed large crowds of people (more than 5,000 at one time) with a few fish and loaves of bread. He called demons out of people. He even brought dead people back to life, including a little girl, a young man, and a grown man.

The friend

Something else special about Jesus was the way he treated women and children. In his day, they were almost like men's belongings. Jesus didn't treat them that way. He was respectful and kind to women and children. He said that people had to become like children to enter God's kingdom. When he was on the cross, he made sure someone would take care of his dear mother.

But Jesus didn't get along with everyone. He criticized religious leaders for thinking they were better than others. They, in turn, didn't like Jesus because he called God his Father and he spent time with people who were not very "religious". The religious leaders came to hate Jesus so much that they had him crucified.

God's plan

Actually, Jesus was born to die. God had planned it before time began. Jesus left his throne in heaven with the purpose of making a way for people to belong to God's family. Jesus was the only human being good enough to die for the sins of the world. Because he is God, he is perfect and sinless. He became a man so he could show people how to live. He died on the cross to pay the penalty for all the sins of all people in all time.

When the time came for Jesus to die, one of his own disciples (Judas Iscariot) betrayed him. Another (Simon Peter) denied even knowing him. The rest of the disciples ran away. Jesus knew all this was going to happen. In fact, the night before he was crucified, he prayed and asked the Father to protect his disciples. Jesus also prayed for all the people who would believe in him in the future.

Jesus' death

Jesus was arrested at night and taken to an illegal trial. He had done nothing wrong, so there was no proper evidence against him. But he was beaten, mocked, and treated like a criminal. Pilate, the Roman ruler, wanted to let Jesus go. But the religious leaders led the crowd in calling for him to be crucified. Pilate didn't want the people to riot, so he gave in.

Crucifixion (death on a cross) was a painful, shameful death. In addition to the physical pain Jesus experienced, he felt all the sin and guilt of all the people in the world for all time. It was such a

The risen Jesus appears to his disciples while they are fishing in the Sea of Galilee.

terrible thing that the sky grew dark and the heavy curtain in the Temple tore from top to bottom.

All the men had deserted Jesus. Only the women who had loved and followed him stayed at the cross until he died. Then two men who had been secret followers of Jesus asked Pilate for his body. They buried him in a cave while the women watched.

Alive again!

But on the third day, early on Sunday morning, some of the women went to put spices on Jesus' body. It was their way of showing care and respect for the dead. To their surprise, the tomb was empty and an angel said that Jesus had risen – just as he had said he would!

The women ran back to the house where the other disciples were. They tried to tell them the Good News about Jesus. At first, no one would believe them. It wasn't until Jesus appeared in the middle of the room without coming through the door that they believed that he had risen.

Jesus appeared to all the disciples at different times, as well as to 500 other believers, before he returned to heaven to prepare a place for his people to live for eternity. He promised to return one day and to take them to be with him in heaven. No one knows when that will happen. He has kept all his promises so far. He will surely keep this promise as well.

MATTHEW

Jesus teaches his followers on a hillside near the Sea of Galilee. This famous talk is called the "Sermon on the Mount".

Four hundred years is a long time to wait for a message from God. That's how long it was between the writing of the last book in the Old Testament (Malachi) and God's next message. After all those years of silence, God finally sent his son, Jesus. The book of Matthew was written by one of Jesus' disciples.

This book is a good link between the Old Testament and the New Testament. It doesn't tell us everything Jesus did and said. But it shows that Jesus fulfills the prophecies about the Messiah, the king of the Jews.

Matthew includes Jesus' genealogy, the list of his ancestors. It goes right back to Abraham to show that Jesus is the one God promised. Matthew makes it clear that Joseph was Mary's husband and that Mary was Jesus' mother, but that God was Jesus' father. Joseph was Jesus' legal, or earthly, father. This showed that Jesus was in the royal line of King David.

The book of Matthew is best known for Jesus' Sermon on the Mount (5–7) and the "Great Commission" (28:18–20). But there are other things in Matthew that mean a lot to Jewish people. They include the visit of the wise men, what Jesus said about the Law and the kingdom of heaven, and Jesus' entry into Jerusalem on a donkey.

Jesus came as king of the Jews. But the people did not recognize him because they thought he would set them free from the Romans. The Jews did not expect their king to be crucified. But Jesus rose from the dead, proving he is God's Son.

OUTLINE

The outline of Matthew is very interesting. It goes back and forth between Jesus' teaching or sermons and his miracles.

Jesus' birth (1–2)

Jesus is born in Bethlehem. The wise men come to worship him, but this puts Jesus in danger, so his parents take him to Egypt.

Jesus' baptism and temptation (3–4)

Jesus is baptized by his cousin John the Baptist, and tempted by Satan. Both events prepare him for his task on earth.

Sermon on the Mount (5–7)

This is one of Jesus' most famous sermons and includes the "Beatitudes".

Jesus shows his power (8–9)

Jesus calms a storm, sends demons into a herd of pigs, heals a bleeding woman, and raises a girl from the dead.

Jesus trains and sends out disciples (10)

Jesus has called his disciples and trained them. Now he sends them out to do his work.

Jesus is rejected (11–12)

The Temple leaders are jealous and scared of Jesus. They start giving him a hard time whenever they can.

Parables about growth (13)

Jesus teaches people by telling them stories. These stories are about a mustard seed, yeast, wheat and weeds, hidden treasure, a pearl, and a fishing net.

Jesus reveals his mission (14–17)

Jesus feeds more than 5,000 people with five loaves and two fish, walks on the water, is transfigured on a mountain, and rescues a boy from demons. Peter declares that Jesus is the Messiah.

Jesus teaches about relationships (18)

Jesus tells the parable of the lost sheep and the story of a man who went to jail because he would not forgive.

Jesus goes to Jerusalem (19–23)

Jesus tells more parables, heals more people, answers questions, and rides into town on a donkey as the crowd cheers.

Jesus teaches about the future (24–25)

Jesus tells about the last days and about when he will come back to earth as King.

Jesus' death and resurrection (26:1 – 28:15)

Jesus says goodbye to his disciples and gives up his own life. God raises him from the dead, and the disciples see him again.

Jesus goes back to heaven (28:16–20)

Jesus commands his disciples to go and make disciples.

Matthew records that Mary and Joseph took Jesus to Egypt for safety.

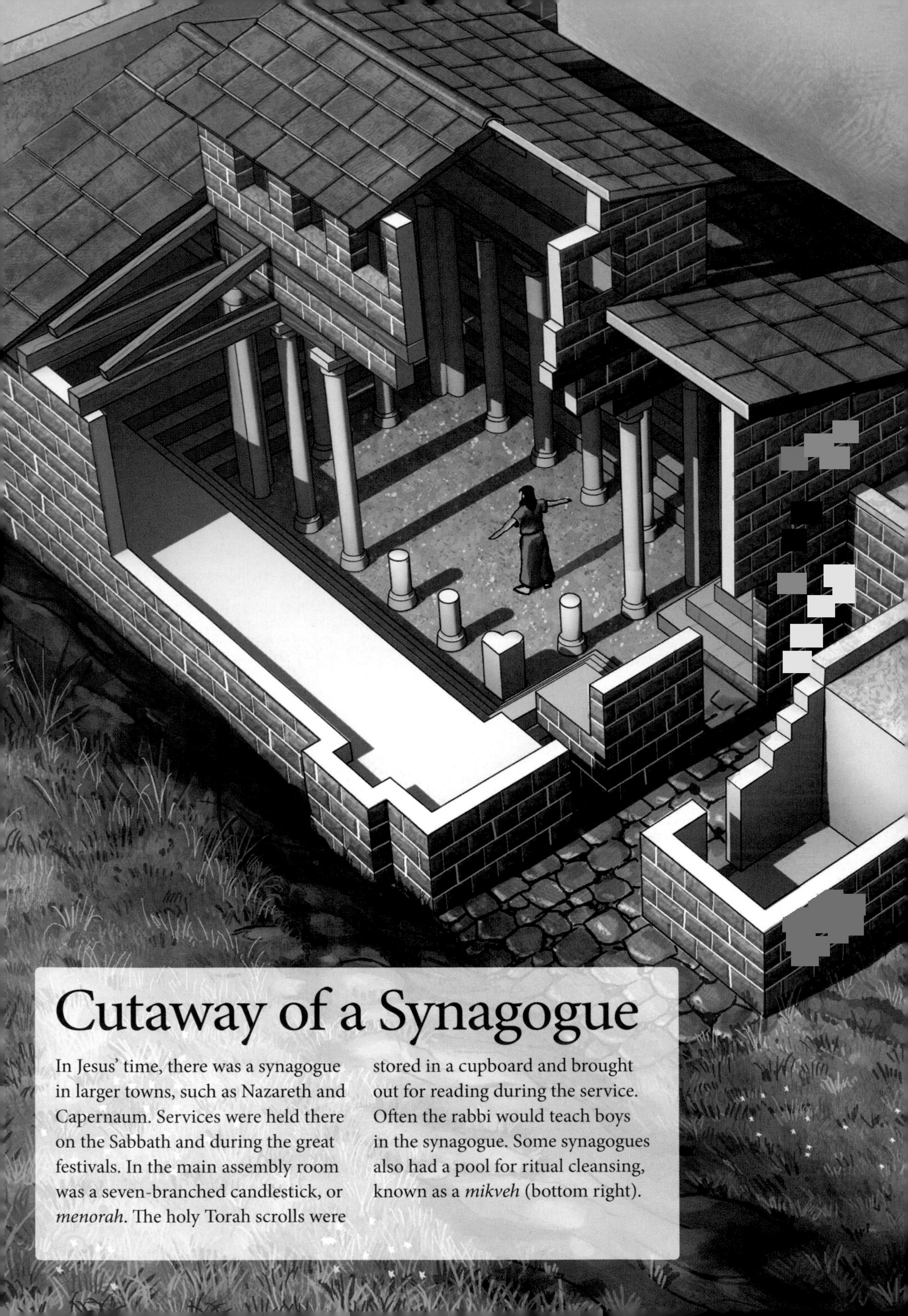

Cutaway of a Synagogue

In Jesus' time, there was a synagogue in larger towns, such as Nazareth and Capernaum. Services were held there on the Sabbath and during the great festivals. In the main assembly room was a seven-branched candlestick, or *menorah*. The holy Torah scrolls were stored in a cupboard and brought out for reading during the service. Often the rabbi would teach boys in the synagogue. Some synagogues also had a pool for ritual cleansing, known as a *mikveh* (bottom right).

Messiah

The Jewish people had been waiting for a Messiah. The Old Testament taught them that God would send someone to save them. The Jews thought God would send a mighty warrior who would fight for them against their enemies. They were disappointed when God's Messiah turned out to be a man who liked to teach them – not fight for them. Jesus was the Messiah they had been waiting for, and he will one day save us from all our enemies.

Look out for...

As you read through Matthew, look out for...

Quotes from the Old Testament. *Matthew quotes the Old Testament more than fifty times and refers to it over seventy-five times!*

Words of Jesus. *Jesus' words are printed in red in some Bibles. Matthew tells us many sermons and stories that Jesus told.*

Kingdom of heaven. *Matthew uses this phrase more than thirty times. Matthew presents Jesus as King.*

Frequently Asked Questions

Q: Why was it important to show that Jesus is the Messiah?

A: God made many promises in the Old Testament about the coming of the Messiah. In the New Testament, Jesus shows that God keeps his promises.

Q: What is the Sermon on the Mount?

A: The Sermon on the Mount is a very well-known part of Jesus' teaching. It includes the Beatitudes, the Lord's Prayer, and the Golden Rule (7:12).

Study Questions

- What did Jesus say about worry? (6:25–34)
- Who is the greatest in the kingdom of heaven? (18:1–5)
- One of the most famous passages in the Bible is Matthew 28:16–20. What makes it so important?

The Miracles of Jesus

The first miracle Jesus did was at a wedding in Cana, when he turned water into wine. After that, he did many other miracles and became much more widely known. Here is a list of Jesus' miracles that are recorded in the Bible.

Healing of individuals

Healing an invalid
John 5:5–9

Healing a girl possessed by a demon
Matthew 15:22, 28; Mark 7:25, 29

Healing a deaf man
Mark 7:32–35

Healing a blind man
Mark 8:22–25

Healing a man who was born blind
John 9:6–7

Healing a boy possessed by a demon
Matthew 17:18; Mark 9:25; Luke 9:42

Healing a blind and dumb man possessed by a demon
Matthew 12:22; Luke 11:14

Healing a woman who had been sick for eighteen years
Luke 13:10–17

Healing a man with swollen legs
Luke 14:2–4

Raising Lazarus from the dead
John 11:43–44

Healing a blind man
Luke 18:35–43

Healing a man's cut-off ear
Luke 22:50–51

Healing a rich man's son
John 4:46–53

Healing a man possessed by a demon
Mark 1:23–26; Luke 4:33–35

Healing Peter's mother-in-law
Matthew 8:14–15; Mark 1:30–31; Luke 4:38–39

Healing a leper
Matthew 8:2–3; Mark 1:40–41

Healing a paralysed man
Matthew 9:2, 6–7; Mark 2:5, 10–12; Luke 5:20, 24–25

Healing a man with a withered hand
Matthew 12:13; Mark 3:1, 5; Luke 6:6, 10

Healing a centurion's servant
Matthew 8:5–13; Luke 7:1–10

Raising a widow's son from the dead
Luke 7:14–15

Healing a man possessed by demons at Gadara
Matthew 8:31–32; Mark 5:1–13; Luke 8:26–33

Healing a bleeding woman
Matthew 9:22; Mark 5:27–29; Luke 8:43–44

Raising Jairus's daughter from the dead
Matthew 9:25; Mark 5:41–42; Luke 8:54–55

Healing a man possessed by a demon who was dumb
Matthew 9:32–33

Miracles involving control of laws of nature

Changing water to wine
John 2:1–11

Catching many fish
Luke 5:4–6

Calming a stormy sea
Matthew 8:26; Mark 4:39; Luke 8:24–25

Feeding 5,000 people
Matthew 14:13–21; Mark 6:30–44; Luke 9:10–17; John 6:1–11

Walking on the water
Matthew 14:25; Mark 6:48; John 6:19

Feeding 4,000 people
Matthew 15:32–38; Mark 8:6–10

Catching a fish with a coin in its mouth
Matthew 17:27

Destroying a fig tree
Matthew 21:19; Mark 11:13–14

Catching a huge number of fish
John 21:5–6

Healing groups of people

Healing two blind men
Matthew 9:29–30

Healing ten men with leprosy
Luke 17:11–19

Healing a crowd in Capernaum
Mark 1:32–34

Healing a crowd by Lake Galilee
Mark 3:7–12

Healing a crowd on a hillside by Lake Galilee
Matthew 15:29–31

KEY EVENTS
Jesus' travels

1. Bethlehem and Nazareth
Jesus was born in Bethlehem. His parents took him to the Temple in Jerusalem to dedicate him. Later, they fled to Egypt to escape King Herod's anger. When it was safe, they returned to Nazareth, where Jesus grew up. At the age of twelve, he went with his family to Jerusalem for Passover and debated with the religious leaders. (Luke 2)

2. River Jordan
Jesus was baptized in the River Jordan by his cousin, John the Baptist. Then the Holy Spirit led Jesus to the desert, where Satan tempted him for forty days. Jesus answered the Devil with Scripture and resisted his temptations. Jesus was ready for his life's work.
(Matthew 3:13–17; Luke 4:1–13)

3. Capernaum
Jesus spent the last three years of his life showing people the kingdom of God. He made his headquarters in Capernaum and journeyed through Israel, preaching, teaching, and healing the sick (Matthew 9:35). He called several of his disciples from their fishing nets on the Sea of Galilee. Near Capernaum, Jesus gave his Sermon on the Mount, including the Beatitudes. (Matthew 5–7)

4. Nazareth
In his home town of Nazareth, Jesus did not do many miracles because people did not believe in him. (Matthew 13:53–58)

5. Sea of Galilee
By the Sea of Galilee, Jesus fed more than 5,000 people with just five loaves of bread and two fish. (Matthew 14:13–21)

Restored remains of the third-century AD synagogue at Capernaum, which almost certainly stands on the site of the synagogue where Jesus taught.

6. Tyre
In Tyre, a Gentile woman asked Jesus to heal her daughter. Jesus was amazed at her faith and did as she asked. (Matthew 15:21–28)

7. Caesarea Philippi
At Caesarea Philippi, Jesus' disciple Peter first declared that Jesus was the Christ, the Son of God. (Matthew 16:13–20)

8. Jericho
The tax collector Zacchaeus lived in Jericho. Jesus went to his house to bring him salvation. (Luke 19:1–10)

9. Bethany
In Bethany, Jesus brought his friend Lazarus back to life. (John 11:1–44)

10. Jerusalem
In Jerusalem, Jesus gave his life for the sin of the world, was buried, and raised back to life.
(John 18–21)

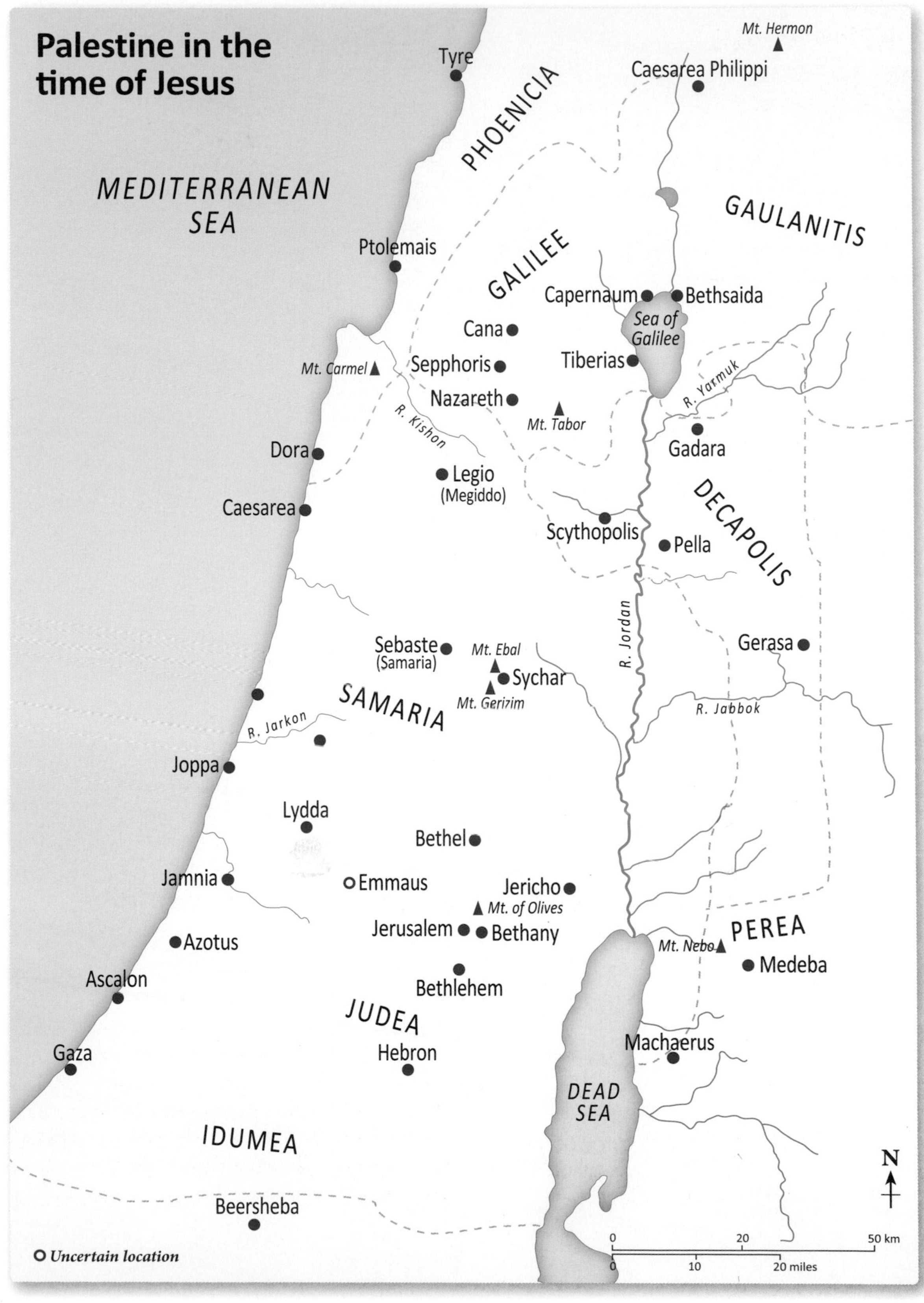
Palestine in the time of Jesus
MEDITERRANEAN SEA
Tyre
PHOENICIA
Mt. Hermon
Caesarea Philippi
GAULANITIS
Ptolemais
GALILEE
Capernaum
Bethsaida
Sea of Galilee
Cana
Mt. Carmel
Sepphoris
Tiberias
R. Yarmuk
Nazareth
Mt. Tabor
R. Kishon
Gadara
Dora
Legio (Megiddo)
DECAPOLIS
Caesarea
Scythopolis
Pella
R. Jordan
Sebaste (Samaria)
Mt. Ebal
Gerasa
Sychar
Mt. Gerizim
SAMARIA
R. Jarkon
R. Jabbok
Joppa
Lydda
Bethel
Jamnia
Emmaus
Jericho
Mt. of Olives
Jerusalem
Bethany
PEREA
Azotus
Mt. Nebo
Medeba
Ascalon
Bethlehem
JUDEA
Machaerus
Gaza
Hebron
DEAD SEA
IDUMEA
N
Beersheba
0
20
50 km
10
20 miles
Uncertain location

Jerusalem in the Time of Jesus

Jerusalem occupied roughly the same area as in the time of Hezekiah, but had expanded to the north and south-west. It was dominated by Herod's Temple, with its impressive courtyards and colonnades (below). Herod the Great had also built for himself a strongly fortified and towered palace (top left), where the Roman governor Pilate resided while in Jerusalem. We know the city also boasted a Roman arena and several pools. A gate from the Temple Mount led directly to the Mount of Olives, probably via a bridge across the Kidron Valley (below). During the great Jewish festivals, the city was thronged with pilgrims visiting the Temple.

MARK

"Action" is the key word for the book of Mark. Mark wrote his Gospel showing what Jesus did more than telling what he said. Mark wasn't a disciple of Jesus, but he was probably an eyewitness of what Jesus did. The Gospel of Mark may be the first of the New Testament books that was written.

The book of Mark is the shortest of the four Gospels. Yet it has more of Jesus' miracles than any of the others. Mark describes Jesus' life, death, burial, and resurrection. He often pictures Jesus as a servant.

Mark was writing to people who were not Jewish ("Gentiles"). They were Romans, Syrians, Greeks, and others who didn't know about the coming of the Messiah. Jesus' actions in helping the sick and needy were meaningful for these people. When Jesus healed people from terrible diseases they could see he had come from the Father.

Jesus wanted to show God's love to people so they would believe in him.

OUTLINE

Jesus is popular in Galilee (1:1 – 3:12)

John the Baptist prepares the way for Jesus and brings him into the spotlight. Jesus begins to gather disciples and heal people.

Jesus makes friends and enemies (3:13 – 7:23)

The Jewish leaders begin to dislike Jesus. They are afraid he will become more important than they are.

Jesus and his disciples (7:24 – 9:50)

Jesus continues to heal people and spends a lot of time teaching the disciples and preparing them for the work they are to do as his followers.

Jesus goes to Judea (10)

Jesus travels to the south. He blesses children and heals more people.

Death and resurrection of Jesus (11–16)

Jesus returns to Jerusalem. He confronts the Jewish leaders and has his last meal (the Last Supper) with the disciples. Then he is crucified. Three days later, he rises from the dead.

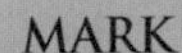

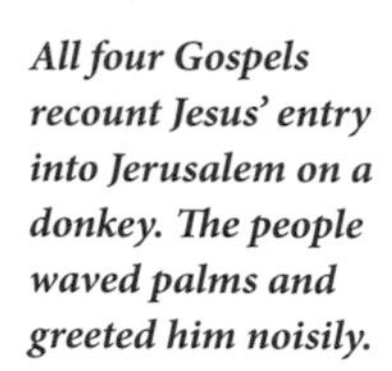
All four Gospels recount Jesus' entry into Jerusalem on a donkey. The people waved palms and greeted him noisily.

Look out for...

As you read through Mark, look out for...

***Explanations.** Mark may have written this book for Christians who were not Jews. Because of this, he explains Jewish traditions and customs.*

***Miracles.** Mark records eighteen of the thirty-five miracles that Jesus did.*

***"Immediately".** More than forty times, Mark uses a word that means "immediately" or "right away".*

Frequently Asked Questions

Q: Why did Mark write his book especially for non-Jewish people?

A: The Holy Spirit inspired people to write the Word of God to meet the needs of different people. The Romans, Syrians, Greeks, and others who were not Jewish might not have understood all the history and promises that God had made to the Jews (see the Gospel of Matthew). But they could understand God's love shown through Jesus' actions.

Q: How did Jesus treat people who were not God's chosen people, the Jews?

A: Jesus wanted everyone to experience God's love and forgiveness. He showed that God cares for Jews and non-Jews alike by healing them, casting out demons, going to their towns and preaching, and sending his disciples to serve them.

Life in Jesus' Time

Jesus grew up in the little town of Nazareth. He would have seen all the activities illustrated here. He often used examples from everyday life – such as farming, grinding grain, or gathering fruit – in his talks and parables.

This is a typical little town of Bible times. The synagogue is top left, next to the olive oil shop. In the middle of the town is the well, where women came to draw water and have a chat. Other people are pressing olives, baking bread, drying fruit, picking olives, making pots, minding sheep, and doing carpentry. The occupying Roman soldiers are keeping an eye on things.

This ancient tomb in Jerusalem has a rolling stone door similar to the door used to seal Jesus' body in the tomb of Joseph of Arimathea. (Luke 23:50–55)

The resurrection

Mark's Gospel ends with the exciting story of the resurrection. Jesus had died on the cross. He had been buried in a stone tomb with a very heavy rock rolled in front of the opening. Mark tells us that three women came to this tomb and found the stone rolled away and an angel nearby. The angel told them Jesus was alive and had gone from the tomb.

The resurrection of Jesus is one of the most important facts in Christian history. Jesus died for our sins. But the fact that he came back to life means he is greater than that sin and greater than death. Because Jesus rose from the dead, we will live forever.

Study Questions

- How did the "Ten Towns" (Decapolis) learn about Jesus' great power and care for people? (5:1–20)
- What did Jesus do for the many people who came to him with problems? (6:53–56)
- How does Jesus want us to pray? (11:20–25)

LUKE

The devout old man Simeon greets baby Jesus as the Lord's Messiah in Jerusalem. (2:22–35)

Angels, shepherds, a stable, and a baby – what could these things mean but Christmas? And where does this best-known and most-loved Bible story come from? The Gospel of Luke.

Luke, the man who wrote this book, was a Greek doctor. He gives many details about Jesus' birth and childhood that none of the other Gospels give. His Gospel shows how Jesus was the perfect man. It's clear that Jesus is God's Son because of the angel's announcement to Mary. But Luke also calls Jesus the Son of Man.

The books of Matthew, Mark, and Luke are called the "Synoptic Gospels". This means "seeing the whole together at a glance". They all tell about Jesus, but from a slightly different angle.

Luke has some details that the other Gospels do not have. For example, Luke records several joyful songs of praise. One of these is Mary's song, known as the "Magnificat", which praises God for what he was going to do for her and through her.

Several parables of Jesus are found only in Luke. They give a clear picture of God's love for the lost. The book of Luke also shows Jesus' tender care for women, who were often mistreated. We learn a lot about Jesus from the book of Luke that we would not know without it.

Luke, author of Luke's Gospel and the Acts of the Apostles, was a physician.

A night-time view of Bethlehem, David's city, and the birthplace of Jesus.

Frequently Asked Questions

Q: **Why is it important that Jesus was a man?**

A: He needed to be a perfect and sinless person to pay for the sins of all people. He faced temptation, just as we do. And he showed us what God is like and how God wants us to live.

Q: **What did the angel tell Mary?**

A: God sent the angel Gabriel to tell Mary she was going to have a baby. But he would not be an ordinary baby born in an ordinary way. The Holy Spirit would form baby Jesus in Mary's womb, even though she was a virgin.

OUTLINE

Jesus' birth, childhood, and roots (1–3)

Luke gives us information about the young Jesus that we cannot find anywhere else.

Jesus teaches and heals in Galilee (4–9)

Jesus teaches and heals around his home town of Nazareth.

Jesus goes to Jerusalem (10–21)

Jesus leaves his home for Jerusalem, the religious capital for his people. The rest of his life is spent there.

Jesus dies on the cross (22–24)

Jesus gives up his life and God raises him from the dead, just as Jesus said he would.

Cleopas and his companion recognize the risen Christ as he breaks bread at supper in their home in the village of Emmaus, outside Jerusalem. (24:13–35)

The humanity of Christ

Jesus was God. But he was also one hundred per cent human. This is hard for us to understand, which is why we call God's humanity a "mystery". Luke's Gospel points out over and over again that Jesus is human.

Luke tells about Jesus' early years, when he grew up just as we do. Luke shows us Jesus' loving care for people as he healed the sick.

Jesus experienced life just as we do, with happiness and sadness. But he was also God, and gave his life so that we could live forever.

Look out for...

As you read through Luke, look out for...

Women. *Luke mentions more women than any other Gospel-writer.*

The poor. *Luke records many of Jesus' words about people who are poor.*

Prayers. *Several prayers are included in the Gospel of Luke.*

Songs. *Luke includes several songs, including Mary's, and the angels' song to Bethlehem shepherds.*

Study Questions

- What are some of the ways in which Jesus showed his special care for women? (7:11–15; 7:36–50; 13:10–17)
- How did Jesus treat children? (18:15–17)

In a parable, Jesus used the familiar activity of sowing seed to teach his followers. (8:4–15)

The Parables of Jesus

Lessons from nature

The sower and four types of soil
Matthew 13:3–8, 18–23; Mark 4:3–8, 14–20; Luke 8:5–8, 11–15

The weeds among the good plants
Matthew 13:24–30, 36–43

The fishing net
Matthew 13:47–50

The tiny mustard seed
Matthew 13:31–32; Mark 4:30–32; Luke 13:18–19

The seed grows by itself
Mark 4:26–29

The seed that died
John 12:24

Yeast
Matthew 13:33; Luke 13:20–21

Signs of the future from a fig tree
Matthew 24:32–35; Mark 13:28–31; Luke 21:29–33

The fig tree that wouldn't grow figs
Luke 13:6–9

The birds of heaven
Matthew 6:26–30

The eagles gather
Luke 17:37

The tree and its fruit
Matthew 7:16

The weather signs
Luke 12:54–56

Jobs and money

The good shepherd
John 10:1–5, 7–18

Wise and foolish builders
Matthew 7:24–27; Luke 6:47–49

The master and the servant
Luke 17:7–10

The good and bad workers
Matthew 24:45–51; Luke 12:42–48

Servants must be watchful
Mark 13:35–37; Luke 12:35–38

Workers in the vineyard
Matthew 20:1–16

The talents
Matthew 25:14–30; Luke 19:12–27

The lampstand
Matthew 5:14–16; Mark 4:21–25; Luke 8:16–18, 11:33

The body's lamp
Matthew 6:22–23

Salt that's thrown away
Matthew 5:13

New cloth on an old coat
Matthew 9:16; Mark 2:21; Luke 5:36

New wine in old wineskins
Matthew 9:17; Mark 2:22; Luke 5:37–38

Hidden treasure
Matthew 13:44

A valuable pearl
Matthew 13:45–46

Treasure from a storeroom
Matthew 13:52

The dishonest manager
Luke 16:1–12

The unforgiving servant
Matthew 18:23–35

The rich man who stupidly built bigger barns
Luke 12:16–21

The rich man and Lazarus
Luke 16:19–31

Wicked renters of a vineyard
Matthew 21:33–44; Mark 12:1–11; Luke 20:9–18

Lost and found

The good Samaritan
Luke 10:25–37

The prodigal son
Luke 15:11–32

Two sons: one obeys, one doesn't
Matthew 21:28–32

The lost coin
Luke 15:8–10

The lost sheep
Matthew 18:12–14; Luke 15:4–7

The shepherd and the thief
John 10:1–18

The doctor and the sick
Matthew 9:12

The sheep and the goats
Matthew 25:31–46

Open and closed doors

The closed door
Luke 13:24–30

The doorkeeper
Mark 13:33–37

The thief in the night
Matthew 24:42–44

A strong man bound
Matthew 12:29

The divided country
Mark 3:24–26

Unclean spirits return
Matthew 12:43–45

The annoying neighbour
Luke 11:5–8

The son's request
Matthew 7:9–11

The widow and the crooked judge
Luke 18:1–8

The Pharisee and the tax collector
Luke 18:9–14

Weddings and feasts

The best man
John 3:28–29

The bridegroom's friends
Matthew 9:15

The unready bridesmaids
Matthew 25:1–13

Invitation to a wedding banquet
Matthew 22:11–14; Luke 14:16–24

The whining children
Matthew 11:16–19

The arrogant guest
Luke 14:7–14

The tower builder
Luke 14:28–32

The rich man and Lazarus
Luke 16:19–31

JOHN

Jesus met the Pharisee Nicodemus by night. He explained to him, "For God loved the world so much that he gave his only Son, so that everyone who believes in him may not die but have eternal life." (3:16, GNB)

Many people say Jesus never claimed to be God. They can't have read the book of John! This book was written by John, one of Jesus' closest disciples.

John was with Jesus more than almost any other person. John was in Jesus' inner circle of friends and saw miracles that few others saw. He saw Jesus' glory when he was transfigured on a mountain. John heard God the Father say, "This is my dearly loved Son, who brings me great joy. Listen to him" (Matthew 17:5). John's message is clear: Jesus is the Son of God.

John lets his readers know that Jesus was the Word of God from the beginning. Jesus is a separate person from the Father, and he is God. Jesus is the Creator who made all that there is.

John reports what Jesus taught about himself. When Jesus talked about himself using the words "I am", he was using words that God used in the Old Testament. Jesus said, "I am the bread of life… the light of the world… the gate… the good shepherd." Jesus was telling people that he is the one who can meet their deepest needs. He is the only one who can forgive sins and bring people into God's family.

John was at the cross when Jesus died. He was also one of the first to see the empty tomb after Jesus rose from the dead.

Anyone who wants to know who Jesus is can read an eyewitness report in the book of John.

The Sea of Galilee at sundown.

OUTLINE

The Word of Life (1:1–18)

John has a beautiful and almost poetic beginning to his Gospel, tracing Jesus' roots all the way back to God himself. This is because John's purpose was to reveal Jesus as the Son of God.

Jesus reveals who he is (1:19 – 6:71)

Jesus reveals himself by calling his disciples, doing miracles, walking on water, talking to a Samaritan woman, talking to Nicodemus, and clearing traders out of the Temple.

Jesus and the Jews (7–12)

Jesus had some enemies among the Jewish leaders. Yet he still tried to explain to them that he was there to help them. He even raised Lazarus from the dead.

Jesus and his disciples (13–17)

Jesus spends some time alone with the disciples. He teaches them and eats his last meal with them.

Jesus dies and rises again (18–21)

Jesus is betrayed by Judas and arrested. He is crucified and buried. Then he rises from the dead and spends more time with his followers before he returns to heaven.

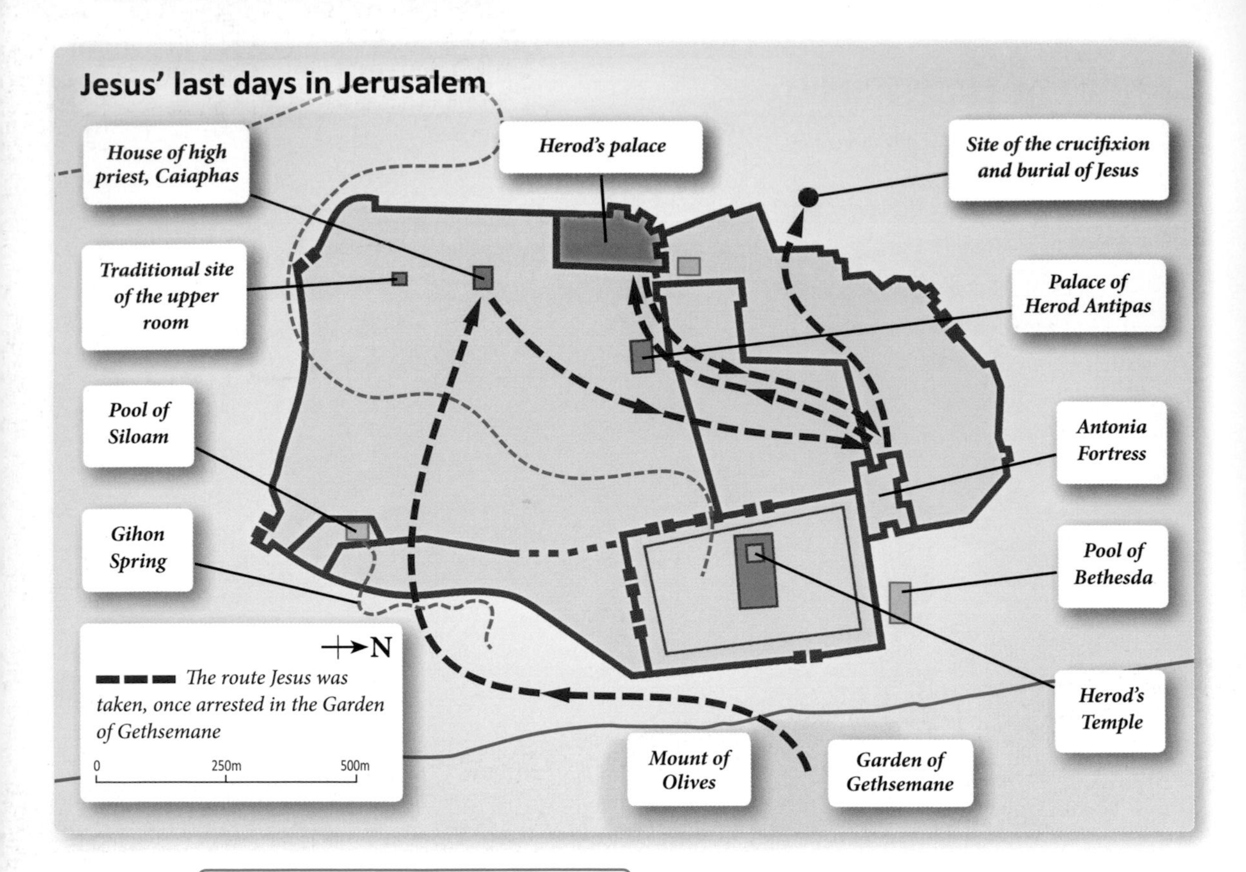

Look out for…

As you read through John, look out for…

Jesus as God. *John says clearly several times that Jesus is God.*

Key words. *John often uses the following key words: witness, believe (almost a hundred times!), light, and love.*

The Holy Spirit. *John is the only Gospel that teaches a lot about the Holy Spirit.*

Word pictures. *John uses word pictures that the other Gospels do not. For example, he calls Jesus the bread of life, the good shepherd, the light of the world, and the way, the truth, and the life.*

Frequently Asked Questions

Q: What does "transfigured" mean?
A: It means that Jesus suddenly looked different. Even though Jesus was God while he was on earth, people did not see his glory. But when Jesus was transfigured, his face shone and his clothes became dazzling white. He shone with the glory that belonged to him as God. John was one of the disciples who saw Jesus' glory.

Q: If the book of Genesis says that God created the world, how can Jesus be the Creator?
A: Because Jesus is God.

Q: Why doesn't John recount everything that Jesus did?
A: None of the Gospel-writers tells us everything Jesus did. But they each give us a picture of Jesus to show that he is God's Son, the Messiah.

Incarnation

Jesus was a human being like you. If he grazed his knee, it bled. He had feelings. He had to learn to read and write. But through a miracle that only God can understand, Jesus was also God. God came to live as a human being. That is called the "incarnation".

This is the only time God has done this. He did it so that we can see that he wants to have a friendship with us. He wants that so much that he took the punishment for our sins on the cross. That was his part in the friendship.

Our part is to believe in him and to trust that he will do what he says. When we pray we are showing that we believe he is listening and that he will answer. That is why John wrote his Gospel – so that we would believe in Jesus.

Study Questions

- What did another man named John say about Jesus? (1:29–34)
- How did Jesus' first miracle help his disciples believe in him? (2:1–11)
- What did Jesus pray for himself? (17:1–5)
- What did Jesus pray for his disciples and all future believers? (17:6–26)

Roman soldiers gamble for Jesus' robe while he suffers on the cross. Pilate ordered that a notice saying "Jesus of Nazareth, the King of the Jews" be put on the cross, overruling the chief priests' objections.

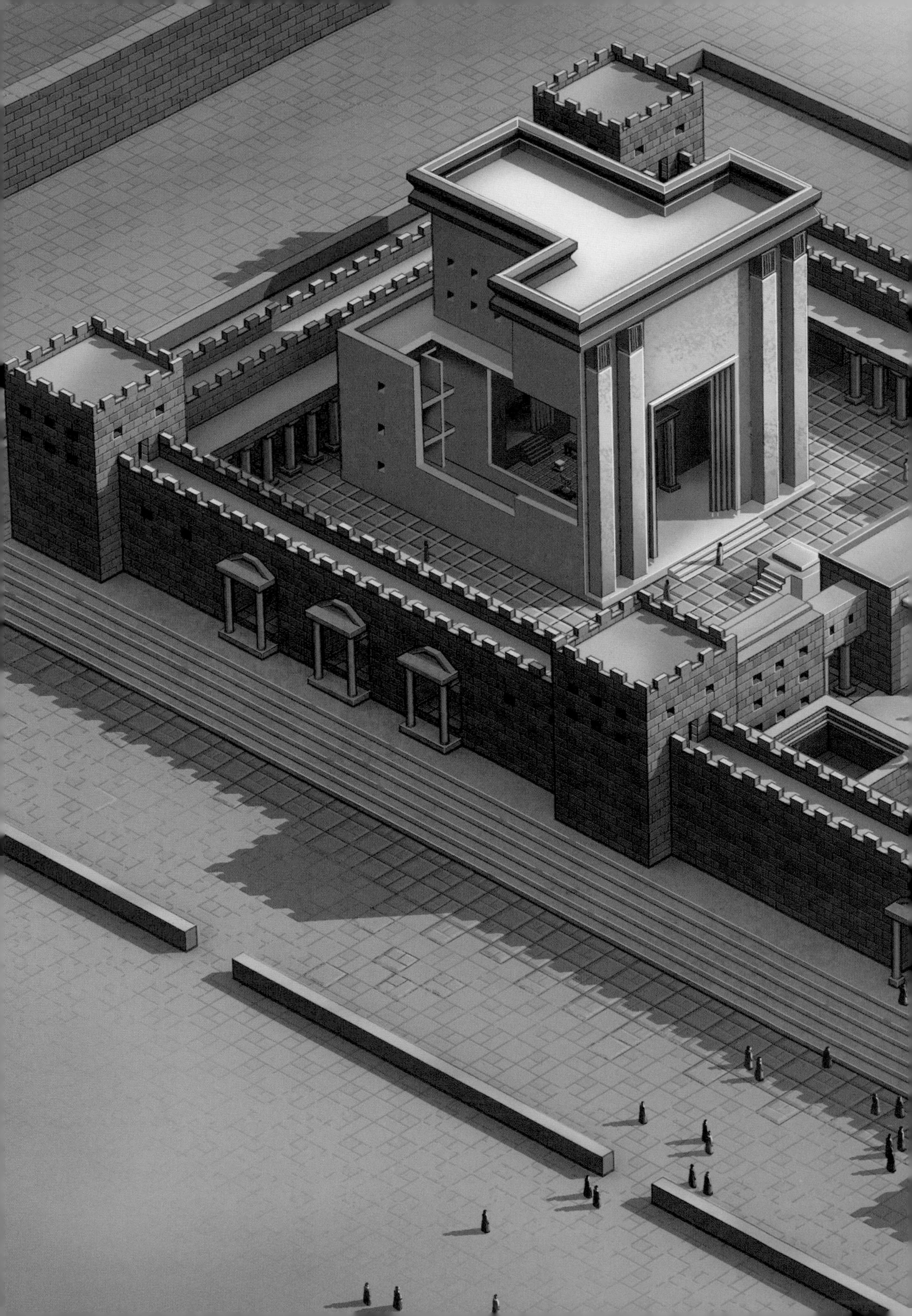

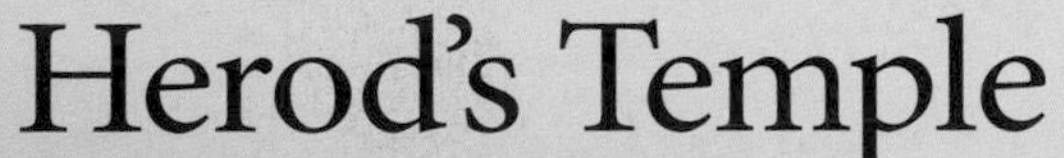

Herod's Temple

Herod the Great started to build the Temple in 20 BC. The central Temple building, like the Tabernacle, consisted of a Holy Place and a Most Holy Place, though the latter no longer contained the Ark of the Covenant. The two areas were divided by a great curtain, which was torn in two when Jesus died. As with Solomon's Temple, a huge altar of burnt sacrifice stood in front of the Temple.

The Temple was surrounded by a number of courts, each more exclusive than the last. Gentiles were only admitted into the outer courtyard. The inner Court of the Women (below) was lit by four huge lampstands.

ACTS

After his conversion, Paul escaped his enemies in Damascus by being let down from the city walls in a basket.

Whatever happened to the scared disciples who ran off into the night when Jesus was arrested? The book of Acts tells the story. It tells what happened after the risen Christ appeared to them and sent the Holy Spirit to help them spread the Good News. It tells of the incredible events that followed after Jesus returned to heaven.

The book of Acts is the history of the early church. It tells how the church began and how it grew and spread from Jerusalem to the Roman world.

The scared disciples became brave spokesmen for Christ. They spoke to the religious leaders. They endured prison, beatings, and even death. But Jesus' message of eternal life in God's family continued to spread.

OUTLINE

Preaching about Jesus in Jerusalem (1–7)

Acts starts by describing the day of Pentecost and the birth of the church. Peter preaches, the apostles heal some people, the church starts, and Stephen becomes the first martyr.

Preaching about Jesus in Judea and Samaria (8–12)

Saul becomes a Christian, the gospel spreads, and an angel rescues Peter from prison.

Preaching about Jesus to non-Jews (13–28)

Paul makes several missionary journeys, is arrested, and taken to Rome.

A highly educated Jewish leader named Saul found out he was working against God. God turned Saul's life upside down. Later, changing his name to Paul, he made three long trips to other countries to tell people about Jesus.

In addition to history, the book of Acts tells what the Holy Spirit taught the Christians. The changed lives of the disciples and of many others, as recorded in Acts, give proof that Jesus Christ is who he said he was – the Son of God.

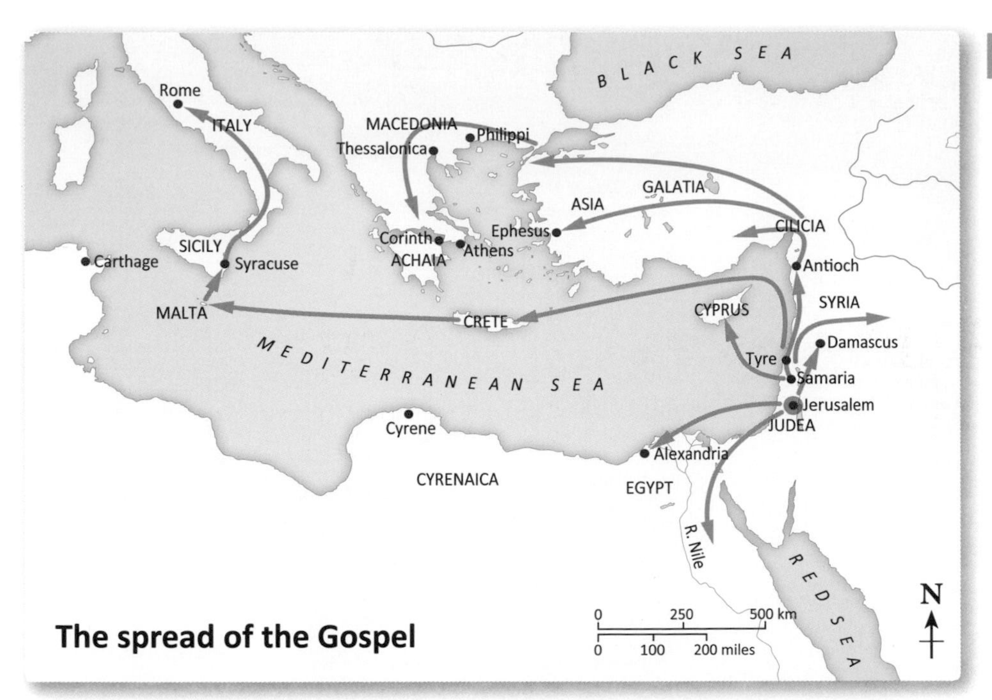

The spread of the Gospel

Pentecost

Pentecost was a Jewish festival that happened fifty days after the Passover. Jesus had been crucified at Passover and was then raised to life. He had appeared to his disciples and then went back to heaven. It was at this festival that the Holy Spirit, the Comforter, first came to live in God's people.

It is important to remember that in the time of Acts, the church was changing fast. God's people were used to praying in the Temple, but Jesus had shown them that God was not just in the Temple. He was in them. They were used to offering sacrifices, but Jesus' death was the final sacrifice anyone would ever need. The coming of the Holy Spirit at Pentecost showed the early church that from then on things would be different.

Frequently Asked Questions

Q: What happened to Jesus' brothers?
A: At first, Jesus' brothers did not believe in him. They taunted him and once they even thought he was out of his mind. But shortly after his death and resurrection, they were in the upper room, along with their mother and other followers, waiting for the Holy Spirit. James, one of Jesus' brothers, later became a leader in the church and wrote the book of James.

Q: Why was the day of Pentecost so important?
A: This was when the Holy Spirit came and filled the followers of Jesus, the first Christians. There was a noise like a loud, rushing wind. Then there were what looked like tongues of fire that rested on each person. These people began to speak in languages they didn't know. Those listening could understand, and many of them became Christians too.

Paul's Missionary Travels

Paul's first missionary journey

Paul, Barnabas, and John Mark were sent west by the church in Antioch. After a while, John Mark left them. Paul always took his message to the Jews first, but usually they didn't want to hear about Jesus. Then Paul would speak to the Gentiles. Paul's life was often in danger. With many Gentiles becoming believers, the church had to decide if they first had to become Jews. Paul taught that faith is what makes someone a Christian – not keeping the Law. (13–14)

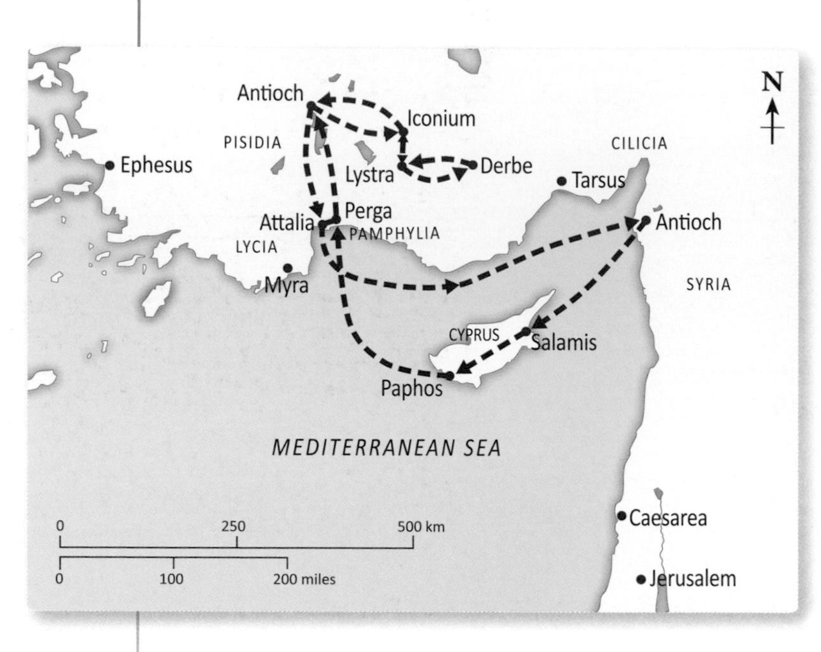

Paul's second missionary journey

Barnabas wanted to take John Mark again, but Paul didn't. They disagreed and went their separate ways. Paul took Silas with him instead to visit the believers in some of the towns he had visited on his first trip. Paul met many people who became his lifelong fellow believers and friends. Best known are Timothy, Lydia, Priscilla, and Aquila. Paul had a vision of a man in Macedonia, asking Paul to help him. On this trip, Paul and Silas were unjustly jailed and God sent an earthquake to rescue them. As a result, the jailer and his family became Christians. (15:36 – 18:22)

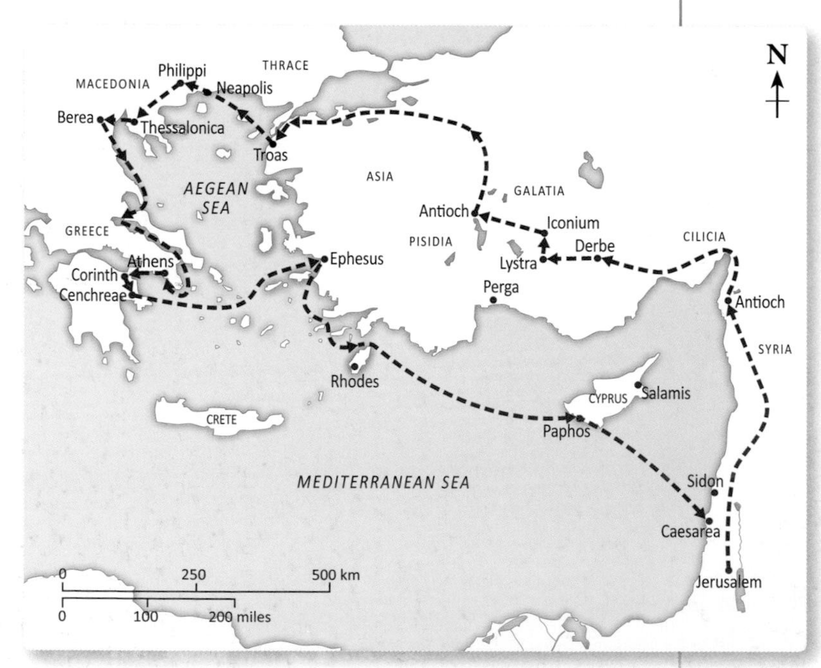

Paul's third missionary journey

Paul returned a third time to the cities he had visited before. Many of his New Testament letters are to churches in these cities. Paul's third trip was to clear up misunderstandings the believers had (18:23 – 20:38). In Ephesus, some men who were silversmiths and made idols of the goddess Artemis caused a riot to get Paul to stop talking about God. Paul said farewell to the elders of the Ephesian church before returning to Jerusalem to report what God had done among the Gentiles. (19:1 – 21:26)

Paul's journey to Rome

When Paul returned to Jerusalem, he was arrested. In an attempt to gain his release, he appealed to Caesar and was sent to Rome. After an eventful voyage, during which he was shipwrecked near Malta, he finally reached the imperial capital, where it is believed eventually he was executed. (27:1–28:31)

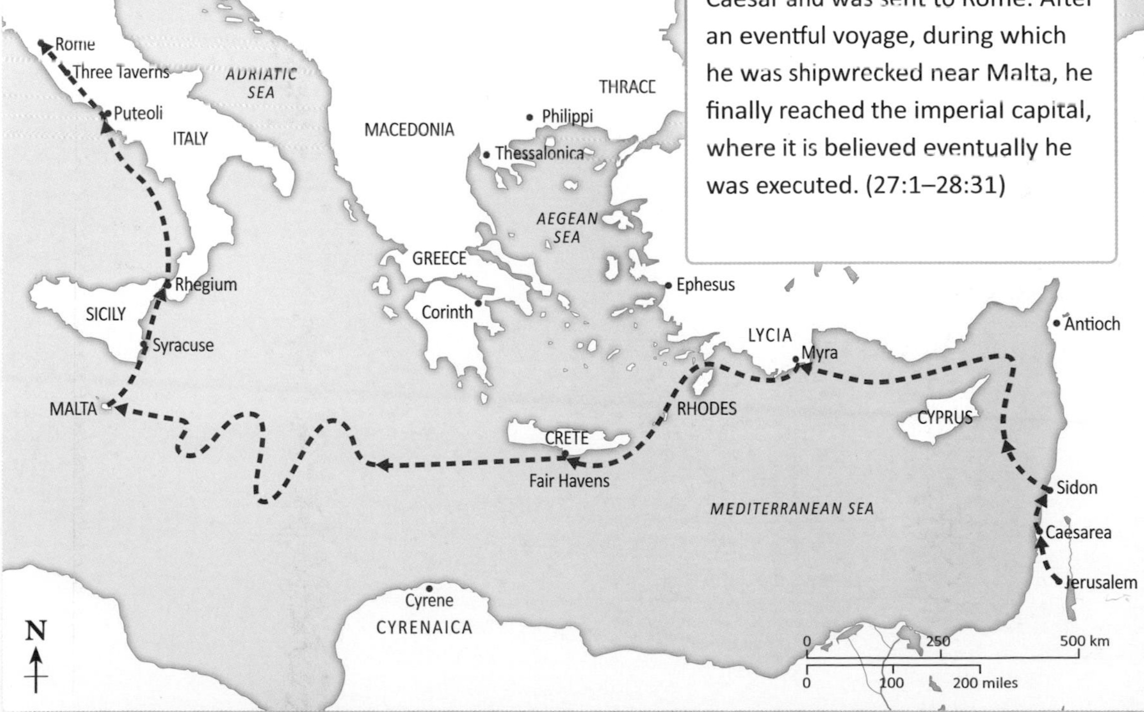

Part of the Roman aqueduct shown in the illustration below is still visible on the beach at Caesarea.

Caesarea

At Caesarea, on the Mediterranean coast of Palestine, Herod the Great constructed the first artificial port of the ancient world. At the entrance stood a lighthouse. The aqueduct that supplied fresh water to the Roman port is still visible. The city was named for Caesar Augustus, and included a hippodrome, an amphitheatre, and a palace for Herod built on a promontory south of the harbour. The Roman governor of Palestine resided here most of the year.

Look out for...

As you read through Acts, look out for...

The Holy Spirit. *Christians get excited because the Holy Spirit comes to be with them, just as Jesus promised.*

Decisions of the early church. *The church leaders have to make many decisions about how they will lead and how they will organize the church.*

Study Questions

- What were Jesus' final instructions to his disciples? (1:8)
- How did God use an earthquake to save a family? (16:16–34)

Athens in the Time of Paul

The temple of the Greek goddess Athena, known as the Parthenon, stands on the craggy hill, or Acropolis. The other hill (top right) is known as the Areopagus, or Mars Hill, and is often said to be where Paul preached a famous sermon (Acts 17:22–34); but it is more likely he spoke in the *agora*, the colonnaded building beneath the Areopagus. Paul's preaching did not win many converts in Athens.

Romans

Titus's Arch, Rome, which was built to celebrate Titus's victories, including the siege of Jerusalem, AD 70. A panel inside the arch depicts the spoils taken from Herod's Temple before it was destroyed.

The apostle Paul had never met the people in the church at Rome. But he had heard about them. He hoped to visit the Christians in Rome on a trip he planned. He wanted to introduce himself and explain the Christian faith to the Roman believers. He wrote to them about what it means to be a Christian.

The letter, or "epistle", that Paul wrote is called the book of Romans. It clearly explains that everyone has sinned because everyone is descended from Adam. It gives the Good News, or gospel, that Jesus Christ died and rose again to pay the penalty for our sin.

The book of Romans also tells about Israel, the church, spiritual gifts, faith, and the Christian life.

It was this book that most helped Martin Luther. In the sixteenth century, the church was teaching that people were saved by good deeds. Luther read in the book of Romans about God's freely given love, "grace". Reading the book of Romans helped Luther trust Jesus. Faith is complete trust.

Other things people can learn from the book of Romans are that Christ can free us from sin, help us to be like himself, and help us live to please him.

OUTLINE

Why Paul is writing (1:1–17)

Paul says he is writing to the Romans to explain the gospel, and what it means for their everyday lives.

We live in a lost world (1:18 – 3:20)

Paul writes to the Romans about the Jewish world as well as the Gentile (non-Jewish) world. He says both worlds need the gospel.

We are accepted by God by faith, not good works (3:21 – 5:21)

Paul talks about many different truths here, but this is his main theme.

Live holy lives (6–8)

Even though we have been accepted by God through our faith, we still have to work to keep sin out of our lives.

The Jews (9–11)

God made some important promises to the Jews, and God is going to keep those promises. The Jews have a special heritage. But salvation is for everyone, not just for the Jews.

Christian conduct (12:1 – 15:13)

As Christians, we are God's representatives. We need to live lives that please him.

Notes from Paul (15:14 – 16:27)

Remember, this is actually a letter. At the end Paul gives some newsy information and says "hello" to friends in Rome.

Inscribed stones in the ruins of the Forum, Rome.

The Forum, Rome, by night.

Look out for...

As you read through Romans, look out for...

Faith. *Paul talks a lot about faith, because many Jews still thought that if they kept enough rules they could please God in that way instead of through faith.*

Sin. *Paul tells us the truth about sin: we all do wrong. We need God's forgiveness.*

Abraham. *Abraham is an important person in this book because he is an example to us all. Abraham did many good things that pleased God, but it was his faith that pleased God most.*

Justification by faith

To be justified is to be found right or righteous. If someone gets angry for a good reason, we say that his or her anger was justified – it was the right way to feel in that situation.

God is holy. That means he is not like anything or anyone else. It also means that he has no evil, no wrong, and no sin in him. Paul's question to the Romans was: "How can we, a sinful people, be justified (right or righteous) to a holy, sinless God?" Paul's answer was: "By our faith in Christ."

When we believe in God, in his son Jesus, and in Jesus' death and resurrection, we are giving God exactly what he wants – our faith. We believe him. We believe in him. That is what he asks of us. We are justified by our faith.

Paul under armed escort by Roman soldiers in the capital city, Rome.

Frequently Asked Questions

Q: How did the people in Rome become Christians?
A: They may have heard the gospel from some Jews who had been in Jerusalem during Pentecost. When Peter and Jesus' other disciples received the Holy Spirit, they spoke freely about Christ. Many people heard the gospel and believed in Jesus. Then they took the Good News back home with them.

Q: What does Adam's sin have to do with people now?
A: Adam is the father of all people. We have all inherited his sinful nature. Even very good people cannot be good all the time and in every way.

Q: How can anyone be good enough to go to heaven?
A: No one but Jesus is good enough to go to heaven. That is why he died in our place and why we need to trust him. Then he gives us his goodness and helps us do what is good and right.

Study Questions

- How did Paul praise the Lord? (11:33–36)
- Since Jesus forgives sins, how should people behave? (12:1–21)

Rome in the Time of Paul

Rome is famously built on seven hills and on the River Tiber. Prominent in the illustration is the great hippodrome, venue for the celebrated chariot races and other sporting events. The Colosseum (the circular building top middle) was built after Paul's death, but many early Christians were martyred there. Many Roman temples are also shown, as well as the Theatre of Marcellus (far left) beside the river.

1 Corinthians

The impressive columns of the Temple of Apollo, Corinth.

The apostle Paul was like a father to the Christians in Corinth. He lived in that city for many months during his second missionary trip. Paul told people how Jesus died and rose again to save them from sin. Many of them believed and became Christians. The book of 1 Corinthians is a letter that Paul wrote to his spiritual children in Corinth.

He wrote it from Ephesus during his third missionary journey. After Paul left Corinth, the people had problems putting their Christian faith into practice. They wrote to him asking for advice. Paul wrote 1 Corinthians to answer their questions and to give them more instructions.

Corinth was a large city by the sea. It had a temple to the goddess Aphrodite. There was a lot of idol-worship, wealth, greed, and immorality in Corinth. Before some of the people became Christians, they lived sinful lives like those around them. After becoming Christians, they were not sure how to live.

So Paul wrote about topics that would help them, such as Christian unity, purity, marriage, spiritual gifts, worship, and future resurrection. He also addressed his letter to "all Christians everywhere – whoever calls upon the name of Jesus Christ" (1:2b, TLB), so that others would learn from it. Christians now and in the future can also learn from the advice and teaching in 1 Corinthians.

Corinth in the Time of Paul

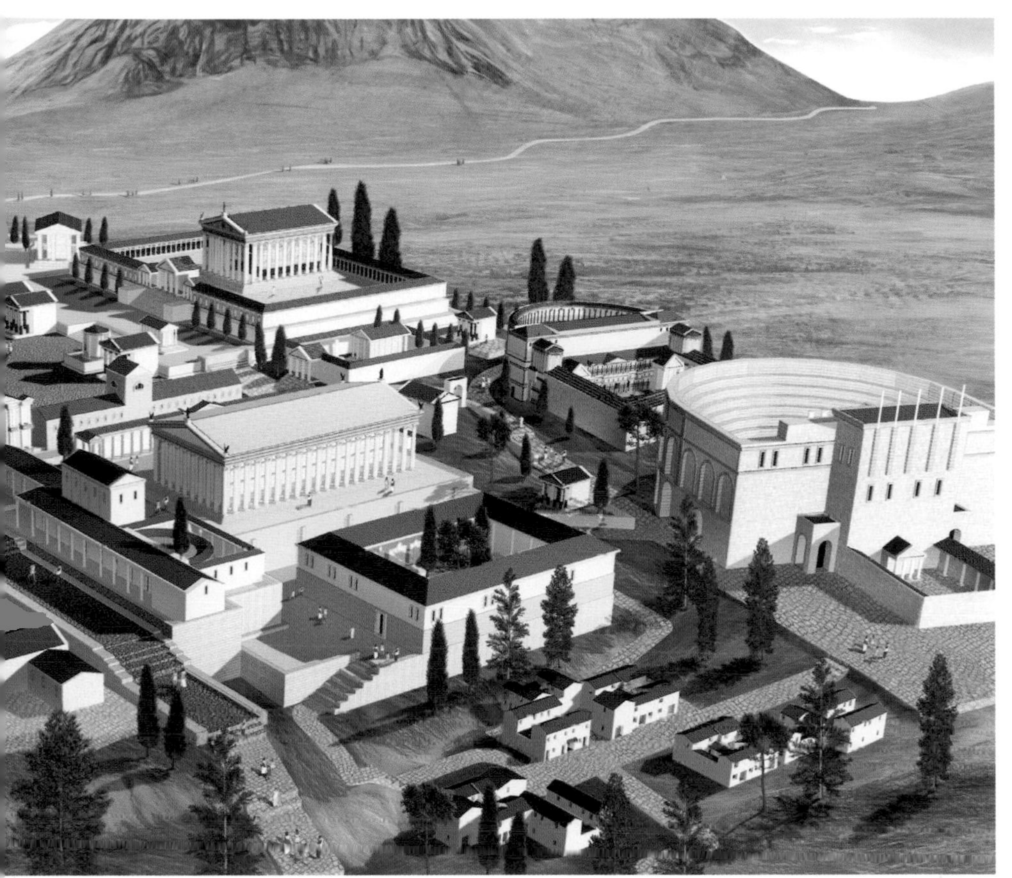

Like Athens, Corinth was dominated by a steep hill, known as Acrocorinth. The city itself boasted all the features of a Greek city of its time, including an amphitheatre and smaller odeion*; the columns of its Temple of Apollo (centre) still stand. The forum, the centre of government of the city and marketplace, is the large enclosed space, middle left. In its centre is the judgment seat, or* bema*, where Paul was probably tried before Gallio. (Acts 18:12)*

OUTLINE

Problems Paul has heard about (1–6)

Paul criticizes the Corinthians' arguments, immorality, lawsuits against each other, and lack of wisdom.

Problems the Corinthians had written to Paul about (7–14)

Paul answers questions about marriage, food, worship, and spiritual gifts.

Resurrection and eternal life (15)

Paul explains the resurrection of Jesus and the resurrection of believers that will happen when Christ comes again.

Personal matters (16)

Paul gives instructions about Christian giving. He also sends them news about people they both know.

Look out for...

As you read through 1 Corinthians, look out for...

Correction. *Paul is writing to correct the Corinthians and help them get rid of sin in their church.*

Sins of the body. *Paul points out many different ways we should be careful with our bodies, especially the food we eat and the way we deal with sex.*

Frequently Asked Questions

Q: What are spiritual gifts?

A: Spiritual gifts are special talents or abilities that God gives to Christians. Their purpose is to bring glory to God and to help other people. The Holy Spirit enables people to use their gifts. Spiritual gifts include teaching, serving, faith, healing, miraculous powers, and prophecy.

Q: Why did Paul talk about Jesus' resurrection?

A: Some people thought Jesus never really died. Others doubted that he came alive again. Paul made it clear that Jesus died, was buried, and rose again, just as the Bible said he would. Paul said that Jesus appeared to Peter, the rest of the disciples, and then to more than 500 people at the same time. Jesus also appeared to his brother James and, finally, to Saul (Paul). If Jesus had not risen from the dead, we would not be able to be forgiven for our sins.

Immorality

Morals are rules about the right way to live. If something is immoral, it is wrong or against the rules. The Corinthians were involved in immorality. Some of their sins were sexual sins. They were also immoral in the way they treated each other. They were not loving or kind. They even took each other to the law court instead of working out their differences.

Paul wrote to them about their immorality so they would change their ways. He told them not to accept immorality in any way. Christians need to have high standards for their lives.

Study Questions

- What's so special about the gospel? (1:18–25)
- Why should a Christian show respect to every other Christian? (12:4–26)
- When is a Christian at his or her best? (Chapter 13)
- How does Paul describe the resurrected bodies that Christians will have? (15:42–57)

2 Corinthians

It is no fun to defend yourself against critics. The apostle Paul did not like doing it either. But he wrote 2 Corinthians to prove that God had called him to be an apostle, just as he had called the original twelve disciples.

This letter was written within a year of 1 Corinthians. Instead of talking about Christian beliefs, it tells of Paul's life and service. It is a very personal letter, telling us how Paul felt about the problems he was facing. There were false teachers in Corinth who were trying to discredit Paul and his message about Jesus.

Even though Paul did not want to defend himself, he reminded the Corinthians of how God had used him to bring them to Christ. He told them how he had suffered for Jesus in order to take them the gospel.

The Corinthian believers were still immature in many ways. Paul encouraged them to believe the truth, instead of believing the false teachers. He did not want to find them living sinful lives the next time he visited them. He loved them and wanted them to live in fellowship with the Lord Jesus.

Another view of the ruins of ancient Corinth. Paul had a great deal to say to the Christians in Corinth.

OUTLINE

Paul's work for Jesus (1–7)

Paul thanks God for his comfort during hardship and tells the Corinthians about some of his decisions.

Gifts (8–9)

The benefits of giving generously and a reminder of what the Corinthians have promised to do.

Paul defends himself against false apostles (10–12)

Paul states his authority and attacks the false teachers who have lied about him.

Closing matters (13)

Paul gives some final advice.

Look out for...

As you read through 2 Corinthians, look out for...

Personal news. *This is a very personal letter by Paul. If you read it carefully, you can learn a lot about him from the things he says about himself.*

Difficult times. *Paul talks about many of his own difficulties and how God has helped him through them.*

Thorn in the flesh

We do not know what Paul meant in chapter 12 by his "thorn in the flesh". We do know it was something wrong with him. He prayed for God to take it away, but God did not. Because of some of the things Paul says in other places, it may have been a problem with his eyes. It affected the way he looked, as well as causing him pain.

But Paul did not let his "thorn in the flesh" hold him back. He still loved people and served them. People sometimes say, "That's my thorn in the flesh." But it shouldn't be an excuse for giving up. Paul's thorn never made him give up.

Paul writes to his Christian friends.

Frequently Asked Questions

Q: How did Paul suffer?
A: Paul suffered beatings, imprisonment, riots, hard work, sleepless nights, and hunger. He even had to be lowered over a city wall in a large basket to escape from thugs.

Q: What were the false teachers teaching?
A: The false teachers were not telling the truth about Jesus. They were teaching about a different "Jesus" and "Holy Spirit". They were saying there was a different way of salvation. They were good speakers, but what they were saying was untrue.

Q: What were the false teachers saying about Paul?
A: These false teachers were saying Paul was not a good speaker. They said he wrote "bold" letters, but was "timid" in person. They said he was weak, and they tried to lure the Christians away from listening to him.

Study Question

- What warnings did Paul give the Corinthian church? (13:1–10)

GALATIANS

Remains of the ancient city of Antioch in Pisidia, visited by Paul. The apostle wrote his letter to the Galatians to the Christians of Antioch and other nearby towns.

The apostle Paul wrote the book of Galatians to help people understand that it's not rule-keeping that makes a person a Christian.

Paul had visited Galatia (now in Turkey). He preached the gospel to Gentiles: people who are not Jews. They put their faith in Jesus and became Christians.

But some other Christians said that faith in Jesus was not enough. They said that all Christians had to keep the Law of Moses in order to be saved. Paul's letter explained that trying to keep the Law of Moses did not save anybody – not even the Jews – because no one can keep the Law. Only faith in Jesus can save a person. So Paul told the Galatians that they didn't need to keep the Law of Moses.

What was true for the Galatians is true for us too: Jesus is the only person who could keep the whole Law. By trusting in Jesus, we become good in God's eyes. It is as if we had never sinned! This was good news for the Galatians – and it's good news for us too.

OUTLINE

Two problems (1–2)

Paul writes to correct two wrong ideas. One is that people must obey the Jewish customs and laws to be children of God. The second is that Paul is not really an apostle.

We are justified by faith (3–4)

Paul spends a lot of time explaining to the Galatians that we become God's children through faith in Jesus, no matter how good we are or how many laws we follow.

We are free in Christ (5–6)

Because we are justified by faith, and not by our good deeds, we are free to be loved by God no matter what we have done.

Remains of the ancient stadium in the city of Perga, visited by Paul during his missionary travels.

Frequently Asked Questions

Q: What were the rules the Jews had to keep?
A: The Jews had many ceremonial laws about worship, food, work, and cleanliness. Paul said God used the Law like a school teacher to show people that they can't be good enough without Jesus.

Q: Did Jesus get rid of the Law?
A: Jesus said he did not come to destroy the Law, but to fulfil it. He is the only one who is perfect and can do everything to please God the Father.

Q: What would have happened if the Galatians had tried to keep the Law?
A: Nothing. It would not have helped them, because no one can be saved solely by keeping the Law.

Look out for...

As you read through Galatians, look out for...

The Law. *Jews have a lot of laws and customs. Paul says a lot about the Christian attitude to those laws and customs.*

Freedom. *Paul wants Christians to have freedom and joy in Christ. He mentions this a lot.*

Faith. *Paul explains faith in many of his letters, and especially in Galatians.*

Jewish religious teachers discuss the Hebrew Torah.

Judaizers

In the Old Testament, God promised Abraham that he would become the father of a great nation. That nation was the Jewish nation. They had many laws and customs and a special relationship with God. God was going to bring the Messiah, Jesus, from that group of people.

But when Jesus died on the cross, he died for everyone's sin, not just the Jews' sin. After Jesus went back to heaven, some of the apostles preached the Good News of salvation not only to the Jews, but also to the Gentiles. This made some people very upset. They believed that a person had to become a Jew, or at least obey Jewish customs, to really be a child of God. These people were called "Judaizers" and were mainly why Paul wrote his letter to the Galatians.

Study Questions

- How should a person use the freedom Christ gives? (5:13–21)
- How should a Christian behave? (5:22–26)

EPHESIANS

The apostle Paul was in jail in Rome for teaching and preaching about Jesus, but his letters were full of good news! The letter to the Ephesians was written to teach and encourage the Christians in Ephesus and other churches nearby.

Ephesians is filled with praise to God for his gift of salvation. It talks about Jesus Christ as the head of all Christians everywhere. Everyone who believes in Jesus is part of his body, the church. Another way to say this is that Christians are in a new family – God's family.

Paul described many of the benefits of belonging to God's family. He also explained to his readers how to live in ways that pleased God. Ephesians has important information about the way people should behave in families.

Paul knew the Devil was real and that Christians were in a battle against him. He encouraged believers to use God's spiritual weapons to fight against the enemy. Today, people still read Ephesians to be encouraged and to learn how to love and respect God.

OUTLINE

Greetings (1:1–2)

Paul usually says who he is, and who he is writing to, at the beginning of his letters.

Beliefs of the church (1:3 – 3:21)

Salvation comes from Jesus, wisdom comes from God, we are alive in Christ, we are one in Christ, we are Christ's body, and God is going to change the world through us.

Actions of the church (4–6)

Paul talks about the importance of humility, gentleness, unity, truthfulness, respect, purity, godly homes, strong families, good workers, and strong people prepared for spiritual wars.

Ephesus in the Time of Paul

Ephesus was a rich port city in the Roman province of Asia. It boasted a famous temple to Artemis (top left) of which almost nothing now remains. During Paul's visit, there was a riotous meeting in the massive theatre when many of the people objected to Paul's preaching. The city also boasted a stadium (near the theatre) and an agora *that served as a marketplace (the colonnaded square near the theatre).*

Look out for...

As you read through Ephesians, look out for...

God's plan for us. *Ephesians tells us a lot about how God wants to use us.*

Personal qualities. *Ephesians lists many qualities that we should show in our lives.*

The church. *Paul tells the Ephesians about the church and what God has planned for it.*

A Roman infantryman with his arms and protective clothing.

Spiritual warfare

A spiritual war is a war against Satan and evil, not against another country or person. Ephesians 6:10–18 is one of the most famous passages about spiritual warfare. It tells us to be prepared. It uses different types of military protection to describe the tools we need to fight evil. Truth is described as a belt. Peace is described as shoes. Faith is described as a shield. Salvation is described as a helmet. The Bible is described as a sword. Prayer does not have a word picture, but is mentioned as an important way to fight evil.

Frequently Asked Question

Q: What's so great about being in God's family?

A: A person who is in God's family is alive in Christ, has God's mercy and salvation, has Christ's power to obey God and to love others, and can call God "Father".

Study Questions

- How do good deeds help a person be saved? (2:8–10)
- What are some of the reasons why Christians should do good deeds? (4:20–24)
- What special advice does this letter have for children and parents? (6:1–4)

PHILIPPIANS

OUTLINE

Greetings and thanks (1:1–20)

Paul is very close to the people in the Philippian church. He thanks God for them.

Suffering for Christ (1:21–30)

Paul has suffered a lot, including being in jail for his faith. Yet he still believes in Christ's mercy and God's goodness.

Living the Christian life (2)

Paul writes about humility, thankfulness, and the examples of Timothy and Epaphroditus.

Knowing Christ (3)

Some people call this Paul's statement of faith. He says that the most important thing in life is knowing Christ and spending every day getting to know him better.

Paul's goodbye (4)

Paul loves these people and takes time thanking them. He also tells them to be strong and happy.

Remains of the theatre in Philippi, Macedonia.

Paul wrote this letter to the church in Philippi. He wrote about his joy while in jail in Rome. He was able to be joyful even when people were against him. He knew that God had allowed him to be in jail so that the gospel could be preached there.

Paul wrote that to follow Christ's example and serve others brings real joy. Paul reminded the church in Philippi that Jesus is the only true source of joy. Compared with Jesus, everything else is worthless.

Paul's letter to the Christians in Philippi was also a thank-you note. They had sent him a gift of money. Paul was glad the Christians wished to share his work. It was their love that gave him joy.

Have you ever been miserable? The book of Philippians can give you a reason to be joyful.

Philippi

Philippi was a city in ancient Macedonia. Macedonia belonged to both the Romans and the Greeks. Its greatest leader was King Philip, father of Alexander the Great. Macedonia was the first part of Europe to hear the gospel, which Paul brought there. He meant a lot to the Christians of Macedonia.

Philippi was an important city. It was probably the home town of Luke, the doctor who wrote the Gospel of Luke. Paul may have visited Philippi on his missionary journey because so many roads went through it. If all of Macedonia was going to hear the gospel, Philippi was a great place to start.

An ancient Greek warrior.

Remains of the ancient prison in Philippi, where Paul and Silas were jailed.

Look out for...

As you read through Philippians, look out for...

The blessing of Christ. *Paul talks a lot about the good things we have because of Jesus' life and death.*

Love. *See all the ways in which Paul expresses his love and encouragement to the Philippians.*

Frequently Asked Questions

Q: Why were some people against Paul?
A: Some preachers were jealous of Paul. They thought they could make trouble for him by preaching too. They also wanted to make a name for themselves. Paul was glad that the message of Jesus was being told – even if some people's motives were wrong.

Q: How did Paul preach the gospel if he was in jail?
A: Paul spoke to the Roman soldiers who were guarding him. People who probably would never have gone to hear him preach heard him every day. Also, other Christians grew brave when they saw Paul's courage in speaking up about Jesus.

Study Questions

- What are Christians supposed to think about and do? (4:8–9)
- How should Christians handle money? (4:11–13)

COLOSSIANS

Gate to the ancient city of Hierapolis, Asia Minor, near the biblical city of Colosse.

For some people, the gospel of Jesus Christ is just too simple. They want to make it complicated. They think there should be "secret knowledge" and special ceremonies that a person must take part in to be saved. The apostle Paul wrote the letter to the Colossians to get rid of that mistaken idea.

False teachers were telling the Colossians that they had to eat and drink certain things and worship in special ways to be Christians. But Paul said that simply having faith in Jesus Christ is what makes a person a Christian.

The false teachers also taught that people needed to worship angels to reach God. But Jesus is the only one we need to reach the Father. Today, many people are interested in angels. Angels are God's messengers – but we are not to worship them.

Another wrong idea the false teachers were teaching is that the body is evil. They even said it doesn't matter what Christians do with their bodies. But Paul explained that God created people's bodies, and that Christians should use their bodies in ways which are pure and holy.

Singing to God, living at peace with others, and doing everything to glorify Jesus Christ are some of the instructions Paul gave to the Colossian Christians. These are also important for believers today.

OUTLINE

Greetings and thanks (1:1–14)
Paul usually explains who he is at the beginning of the letter. Here he also gives some news, just as you would if you were writing to a friend.

Christ is above everything else (1:15–29)
The Colossians need to understand that Christ is God, only Christ died for our sins, and only Christ is worthy of our worship.

What to believe (2)
Several false teachings are discussed. Some people worship angels. Some people put too many harsh rules on themselves. Some people are too proud. Paul talks about each of these problems.

How to live in Christ (3:1 – 4:6)
This is the Good News. Paul points out that since Christ is above all and has forgiven our sins, we have wonderful lives to live. We also have a responsibility to make wise choices and to love one another.

Final goodbyes (4:7–18)
Paul finishes his letter much as you would. He gives some more news and some instructions.

Frequently Asked Questions

Q: Why did Paul remind the Christians that Jesus is God?
A: False teachers were saying that the body is evil, so God would not have come in bodily form. Paul made it clear that Jesus was both God and man at the same time.

Q: Why did the false teachers want people to have special ceremonies and rules?
A: The false teachers wanted their own religion because it made them feel important.

Look out for...

As you read through Colossians, look out for...

Titles of Christ. *Paul uses a lot of different titles for Jesus, because Jesus does and is so many things in our lives.*

Doctrines and beliefs. *Paul is writing to correct some false teachings. Because of this you will find a lot about different beliefs.*

Instructions to families. *Paul tells us some ways to be good family members.*

Quayside scene at a Mediterranean port in Roman times. Paul would likely have sailed in a trading vessel of this kind.

Study Questions

- What instructions did Paul give for Christian living? (3:1–17)
- How are Christian families supposed to live? (3:18–21)

1 Thessalonians

Paul wrote two letters to the Christians at Thessalonica. This is a panel from a relief picturing an offering at a pagan altar, from the Arch of Galerius in Thessalonica.

The church at Thessalonica was a young church. It began as a result of Paul's preaching during his second missionary trip. About two or three years later, he wrote the letter now called 1 Thessalonians.

Paul told the believers that he prayed for them often. He encouraged them to continue in their faith in Christ. He reminded them how he had lived and worked with them, and how much he loved them. Paul said he was like a mother to the believers, and he missed them.

The city of Thessalonica was an important, busy place. Idol-worship was common there, and Christians were persecuted. Paul wanted to know whether the believers remained faithful to Christ. He sent his friend Timothy to encourage them. Paul was encouraged to learn they were still following the Lord.

But one thing troubled the Christians: they didn't understand why it was taking Jesus so long to return. Paul told them that no one except the Father knew when Jesus would come back. Paul's advice was that they should continue living holy lives to please God.

The Thessalonians were also concerned about the people they loved who had already died. Would those who had died miss Jesus' return? Paul told them that believers who died would be the first to rise and return with Jesus. The job of those who are still alive is to live pure and peaceful lives.

OUTLINE

The conversion of the Thessalonians (1)

When the Thessalonians came to believe in Christ, they followed him wholeheartedly.

The beginning of the church in Thessalonica (2)

Paul shares his memories of when he and Silas helped start the church.

Paul's concern and instruction for the church (3:1 – 4:12)

Paul is concerned about the suffering the church has gone through.

Jesus' return (4:13 – 5:11)

Paul explains that Christians who have died will be raised to life when Jesus comes back.

Paul's final instructions (5:12–28)

Paul reminds them to love each other and live for Christ.

Frequently Asked Questions

Q: Why didn't Paul go himself to see the Christians in Thessalonica?
A: Paul said that Satan stopped him from going back to Thessalonica (2:18). He doesn't explain what happened or how Satan prevented him from returning.

Q: Who was Timothy?
A: Timothy was a fellow worker with Paul. He often accompanied Paul on his missionary trips. Timothy sometimes carried letters from Paul to other believers.

Look out for...

As you read through 1 Thessalonians, look out for...

Jesus' return. *Paul writes a lot about this. Notice that chapters one to four all close with comments about the return of Christ.*

Paul's instructions. *Paul reminds the Thessalonians several times how they are to treat each other and live for Christ.*

The second coming

When Jesus came to earth to die for our sins, he was born into the world as a baby. That is called the "incarnation". The next time Jesus comes to earth, he will come as a king to take us home to heaven. This is called the "second coming".

The Thessalonians had many questions about the second coming. That's one of the main reasons Paul wrote this book and 2 Thessalonians. We are still looking forward to the second coming. The Bible tells us in many places, including the Thessalonian letters, to live holy lives so we can be ready to meet Christ face-to-face when he comes.

Study Question

- What encouragement did Paul give the Thessalonians about the second coming of Jesus? (4:13–18)

2 Thessalonians

Remains of the ancient Roman forum at Thessalonica, which Paul would have visited. (Acts 17:1–9)

Some of the Christians in Thessalonica were confused about the second coming of Jesus. They misunderstood Paul's first letter to them. They thought Paul had told them Jesus would come back any minute. They decided to stop everything they were doing and just wait. Paul wrote a second letter to the Thessalonians to help them understand what he actually meant.

He was glad they believed in Jesus, but he did not want them just to sit and do nothing. Some people were not even working to provide for their families. Instead of being busy at work, they wasted time and chatted.

The advice Paul gave was strong. He said, "Whoever doesn't work shouldn't eat." Paul said the believers should warn other believers who were refusing to work.

Paul wanted the Christians to watch and work while waiting for Christ's return. This letter gives believers today good advice about how to live while waiting for Jesus to come again – work hard!

OUTLINE

Greetings and thanks (1)

The Thessalonians stood strong during persecution and Paul tells them so.

The second coming (2)

Paul tells the Thessalonians not to worry that the end has begun, and tells them signs of Jesus' coming.

Instructions and helpful words (3)

Paul encourages the church to keep busy by doing good.

Look out for...

As you read through 2 Thessalonians, look out for...

Signs of the second coming. *Particularly in chapter two, Paul explains these signs, so that we can be prepared.*

Persecution. *Some people were harassing Christians, just because they were Christians. Paul wrote encouraging words to these Christians.*

Frequently Asked Questions

Q: Why did the Thessalonians think Jesus was coming any minute?
A: A lot of Christians were in big trouble with the government. Roman officials didn't like Christians and were allowed to hurt them, harass them, and even kill them just for being Christians. So the Thessalonian Christians thought that Jesus would be returning any minute to rescue them.

Q: What should we do while waiting for Jesus to return?
A: We should do everything God has told us to do. We should work at our jobs, obey God, serve him, take care of our families, tell others about Jesus, help the needy, pray faithfully, love others, build up the church, and do good.

The antichrist

John mentions the antichrist in 1 and 2 John. While this is the only time the actual word is used, Paul is talking about the same person in 2 Thessalonians 2:8 when he talks about the "man of lawlessness". In fact, ever since Old Testament days, God's people have known about a person or power at the end of time who will attack them. That attack will be crushed by Jesus, the Messiah.

Paul wanted the Christians in Thessalonica to understand that the antichrist had not come yet, so Christ's coming was not about to happen in the next days or weeks. He gave them a sign to look for so they would continue working until Christ came.

Study Question

- What did Paul say would happen before Jesus Christ returns? (2:1–12)

A Roman oil lamp, made of clay.

1 TIMOTHY

When the apostle Paul was older, he wrote to Timothy to give him advice. Timothy was a young pastor. Paul wanted Timothy to do a good job leading the church at Ephesus. Paul wrote to him about what was important. His letter is called 1 Timothy. It has good advice for church leaders and other Christians even today.

Paul said that doctrine – what people believe – is very important. He didn't want Christians to get muddled and believe lies about Jesus or about being a Christian. He told Timothy to pray for rulers so that Christians could live peaceful lives.

Paul also said the life of the church is very important. He advised Timothy how believers should worship God. He also gave instructions about choosing church leaders. Churches are made up of all ages of people, and of people in different circumstances. Paul advised Timothy how to treat people kindly, yet firmly. This letter is a good guidebook for any Christian learning to serve God and God's people.

Born to a Jewish Christian mother and Greek father, Timothy became an important friend and helper to Paul.

OUTLINE

Greetings and instruction (1)
Paul asks Timothy to stay at Ephesus and deal with the teachers who aren't doing right.

Instructions for worship (2)
Paul urges the people to pray and prepare for worship.

Instructions for church leaders (3)
Church leaders must live holy and respectable lives.

How to handle false teachers (4)
Timothy should take a stand against false teachers by teaching the truth.

How to treat each other (5:1 – 6:2)
Treat elders with respect and take care of widows.

Riches and a godly life (6:3–21)
People should concentrate more on loving God than on getting money.

Elders and deacons

Elders and deacons both served as church leaders in Timothy's day. Elders were also called "bishops" or "overseers". They were to have good reputations and live blameless lives. Their job in the church was to keep an eye on the spiritual growth of the congregation and the teaching of God's Word. Today, some churches have several elders; others have just their pastor as an elder.

The first deacons took care of feeding the church, so the apostles had more time to teach. Today, the deacons sometimes help make decisions in the church.

Look out for...

As you read through 1 Timothy, look out for...

Worship guidelines. *Paul tells Timothy how to lead the church in worship.*

Advice and instructions. *Paul is a friend and teacher to Timothy, so he gives him a lot of great advice.*

Reasons. *Paul doesn't just tell Timothy what to do. He also tells him why he needs to do it that way.*

A view of the site of ancient Ephesus from the top of the huge amphitheatre, which the apostle Paul knew from his visit. In his time, the sea came as far as the green area at the far end of the marble roadway, where the quay was situated.

Frequently Asked Questions

Q: Why did Paul think he should give Timothy advice?

A: Paul and Timothy were close friends. Paul thought of Timothy as a son. Timothy helped Paul in his ministry. Paul knew that being a pastor is a big responsibility and wanted to encourage Timothy.

Q: Why is it important to pray for government leaders?

A: If government leaders do good, everyone benefits. They make good laws and make it easier for everyone to lead a peaceful life.

Study Questions

- What kind of people should be leaders in the church? (3:1–13)
- How did Paul say that Timothy should treat the various people in the church? (5:1–21)

2 Timothy

Paul was imprisoned in Rome, but still able to write lengthy letters to churches and to his believing friends.

OUTLINE

Be faithful (1)

Paul tells Timothy to live his life by the good teaching he has received. We need to do the same thing.

Be a good soldier (2)

Work hard for Christ, being faithful during hard times and staying away from silly arguments.

The last days (3:1–9)

Be ready for difficult times. Some things will get worse as the world gets older.

Paul's goodbye (3:10 – 4:22)

Paul tells Timothy to be strong for God. He also tells Timothy some news, and who Timothy should say "hello" to – and he asks Timothy to visit him soon.

The apostle Paul was in prison waiting to be executed for his faith in Christ. Paul wrote his last letter to Timothy. It's in the Bible as 2 Timothy. Paul loved Timothy like a son. He wrote to Timothy to remind him how to be a good pastor.

He encouraged Timothy to remain true to his teachings about Christ. Paul told Timothy to pass on to other faithful Christians the Good News about Jesus. Then they could teach others. That is how we have received the message of Christ down through the ages.

One of the main things Paul told Timothy to teach was that Jesus was completely God and completely man at the same time. Paul warned that many people would not want to hear the truth – but Timothy was to continue teaching God's truth anyway.

Paul also showed his great love for the Bible. He told Timothy that the Bible was inspired by God. It is a guidebook showing Christians how to live a Christian life. Paul asked Timothy to visit him in prison and bring his "papers" to him. The papers were probably copies of Old Testament books. It was through reading and knowing God's Word that Paul built up his faith in Christ.

Paul's imprisonment

Paul wrote this letter when he was in prison, waiting to be executed. He had not done anything wrong. He was in prison for telling others about Jesus. He had been under arrest once before, but had been released. This time he had no reason to believe this would happen.

Paul didn't have many visitors. People were afraid to come to see him. So Paul was alone in prison, probably in chains, waiting to die. But he didn't just get depressed and give up. He wrote to Timothy so that Timothy could continue the work that Paul had started.

That is what makes this letter special. Paul told Timothy the things that were most important to him because he knew that it might be one of his last chances to do this. Paul wrote so that Timothy would be strong. We can read this letter and be strong too.

Look out for...

As you read through 2 Timothy, look out for...

Advice. *Paul writes this letter to give Timothy important advice. It's good advice for us too.*

Difficult times. *Paul has been through some rough times: jail, beatings, huge disappointments, and now prison. He tries to prepare Timothy for similar troubles.*

People. *Paul mentions twenty-seven different people in this letter. This is more than in any other letter of Paul's.*

Study Questions

- What did Paul say people will be like in the last days? (3:1–5)
- How did Paul describe the Bible? (3:16)
- How did Paul face his coming death? (4:6–8)

Frequently Asked Questions

Q: What proof did Paul give that Jesus was both God and man?
A: Paul reminded Timothy that Jesus rose from the dead and was descended from King David.

Q: Why didn't Paul have his papers with him in prison?
A: Paul was probably arrested and taken to prison in a hurry and couldn't take his things with him.

TITUS

Paul was facing execution because of his faith in Jesus. Titus was a Greek believer who had journeyed with Paul on some of his missionary trips. When Paul needed a strong leader for the churches on the island of Crete, he sent Titus. He told Titus to help the believers build a strong church.

The letter Paul wrote to Titus is called the book of Titus. It is the third letter to a pastor (the others are 1 Timothy and 2 Timothy).

Titus also needed help in serving the church. Paul gave him advice about what sort of people should be leaders. He made it clear that church leaders have to be people who study God's Word. They must also follow Jesus. Titus would have to be on his guard against false teachers.

Paul gave Titus other instructions too. He told Titus how the believers should live. Once a person is a follower of Christ, he or she should want to do what is right and pleasing to God.

Titus was a Gentile Christian and friend and helper of Paul.

OUTLINE

Church leaders (1:1–9)

Church leaders should be loving people who consider God in everything they do.

False teachers (1:10–16)

Church leaders should warn their people about false teaching.

Right living in the church (2)

We need to teach each other and do what is right.

Right living in society (3)

When we obey the law of the land, we help others see God living through us.

Frequently Asked Questions

Q: Why did the churches on Crete need strong leaders?

A: The people of Crete were known as lazy and undisciplined. The Christians there needed extra help to become good workers. This would make them good examples of how God can change people.

Q: Are there any other letters to church leaders like Titus?

A: The books of 1 and 2 Timothy are also letters to a church leader.

Balos beach, Crete.

Crete

Crete is an island just south of Greece. It was a large and prosperous island with almost one hundred cities when Paul was alive. Paul and his friends had started churches in many of those cities. But when Paul left, someone was needed to help those people grow as Christians.

Paul tells Titus that the people of Crete were described as liars, lazy, and cruel. Titus had a tough job helping the people of Crete to follow God and obey him, rather than live the way most Cretans did. But Titus had worked with difficult people before, and that may be why Paul sent him to this troubled place.

Look out for...

As you read through Titus, look out for...

Christian leaders. *Paul wrote to Titus to describe the qualities a Christian leader needed.*

Grace and salvation. *Paul says we should live godly lives to gain God's grace and salvation.*

Study Questions

- What should church leaders be like? (1:6–9)
- What were the false teachers like? (1:10–16)
- How should Christians live? (2:1–15)

PHILEMON

Onesimus the slave presents his master, Philemon, with Paul's letter.

OUTLINE

Paul's greeting (1:1–3)

As usual in Paul's letters, he starts out by saying who he is and who he's writing to.

Paul speaks well of Philemon (1:4–7)

Philemon has been a loving and kind person.

Paul's special request for Philemon (1:8–21)

Philemon should forgive Onesimus because God commands us to love and forgive others.

Paul's goodbye (1:22–24)

Paul mentions some friends.

Philemon was probably a rich Christian: the church met in his home and he had slaves. Paul wrote to ask Philemon to forgive his runaway slave, Onesimus. Onesimus had fled to Rome, and had then met Paul and become a Christian.

Paul told Philemon he prayed for him and thanked God for Philemon's love for believers. Then Paul told Philemon that his slave Onesimus had become a believer. Paul asked him to accept Onesimus back as a brother. Paul appealed to Philemon's love for him.

Look out for...

As you read through Philemon, look out for...

Reasons. *Paul gives Philemon various reasons for showing kindness to Onesimus.*

Study Question

- How did Paul think Philemon would respond to his request? (1:21)

A troop of men in Roman military costume.

Slaves

Slaves were common in the Roman world of Paul's time. Some people sold themselves into slavery to pay off debts. Some of them were treated more like servants than slaves. Many young girls were sold to be maids and to take care of a household or of children.

Laws governed the treatment of slaves, but some slaves were still badly treated because they were regarded as property. Paul didn't try to abolish slavery. Instead, he pointed out that God made us all, and that we should love everyone, no matter who they are.

A Roman slave badge.

Frequently Asked Questions

Q: Why did the church meet in Philemon's house?
A: He was a kind and generous man who wanted to help the church. They didn't have a church building, so they met in Philemon's house. Most early churches gathered in private houses like his.

Q: Why did Philemon have a slave?
A: Slavery was common at this time. Paul asked Philemon to receive Onesimus back as a brother rather than a slave.

Hebrews

The book of Hebrews was written to Jewish Christians who were wondering if it might be better to return to their old Jewish faith. They were first-century Christians who may have been puzzled why Jesus had not returned yet to set up his kingdom.

The writer of Hebrews makes it clear that everything about Jesus Christ is better than any other leader or religion. Jesus is superior to the prophets, angels, Moses, the Jewish priests, and the whole Old Testament way of serving God. Jesus is better because he is God.

The writer of Hebrews said that the people should have been mature Christians by the time he wrote the letter, but that they were still like babies needing milk. He encouraged them to do good, so they would be strong and resist when tempted.

The book of Hebrews is probably best known for chapter 11. Many believers of the past are listed in this "Hall of Faith". For 2,000 years it has encouraged Christians to trust in God.

Christians today can read the book of Hebrews and be reminded to stay true to Christ because he is the best.

OUTLINE

Christ is above everything else (1:1 – 4:13)

Christ is greater than the angels and greater than Moses.

Jesus as priest (4:14 – 10:18)

Jesus is the greatest high priest who has ever lived and ever will live.

Christians must endure (10:19 – 12:29)

Examples of people who believed in God – "had faith". People are encouraged to hold on to their faith, no matter what.

Goodbyes and personal notes (13:1–25)

The writer encourages believers to live obedient lives.

Look out for...

As you read through Hebrews, look out for...

Faith facts. *Hebrews talks a lot about people with faith and how God responds to their faith.*

Characteristics of Jesus. *Hebrews talks about Jesus' many different roles, including those of prophet and priest.*

God's love. *Hebrews reminds us that God loves and cares for us.*

The high priest hears a case in the Jewish religious court, the Sanhedrin, at the Temple in Jerusalem (see Matthew 27:1, Acts 5:21). Notice the scribe at the table making a record of the case.

Frequently Asked Questions

Q: Why would Jewish Christians want to give up their faith in Jesus?

A: Everybody thinks fondly of the past sometimes. That is what these Jewish Christians were doing. They remembered the old ways and wondered if they were all right after all. God had revealed himself to the Jewish (Hebrew) people in the Old Testament; they were special to him. But the Jewish Christians were forgetting that Jesus is more important than anything else.

Q: How does Hebrews say that Jesus is best?

A: Hebrews reminds us that angels are God's messengers, but Jesus is God's Son. Prophets told about the Messiah coming: Jesus is the Messiah. Priests had to sacrifice daily for sin, but Jesus sacrificed himself once for all sin.

Herod's Temple, covered in white marble and decorated in gold, glittered in the bright sunlight of Jerusalem.

Faith

Hebrews connects the Old Testament to the New Testament through faith in Christ. The writer of Hebrews gives many examples of people in the Old Testament who believed in Jesus even before he came to earth. They believed because they read in the Old Testament that Christ was coming. They were saved by trusting in God, just as people are saved today because Jesus died and rose again once for all sins of all time.

Hebrews also encourages us to have faith. As you read the New Testament, and especially Hebrews, you can look back on Christ's life, just as the Old Testament believers looked forward to Christ's life. It is faith in Christ that ties the whole Bible together.

Study Questions

- How was Jesus a high priest? (9:11–14)
- What did God do for the people in the Old Testament who stayed faithful to him? How do we have a part in his promises? (11:1–40)

JAMES

We don't naturally thank God for trouble. Usually, we do whatever we can to avoid it. But the book of James starts with advice to let trouble be an opportunity for joy (1:2).

The people to whom James was writing were Jewish Christians living among Gentiles. Many of them suffered for being Christians. Non-Christians would harass and mock them for it. James told his readers that these troubles could teach them to grow strong in Christ. That's why he said they should be thankful for their problems.

The book of James teaches that faith is shown by actions. A person shouldn't just say he or she is a Christian, but live like one. A Christian should want to live the way Jesus says people should live. After all, God loves us so much he sent Jesus to die for us.

James wrote that our words show what we are like. We can ask God for wisdom, and he will help us to know how to speak to others.

The book of James also teaches that we shouldn't let a person's riches or poverty affect our attitude to him or her. We should be kind to all people equally.

The book of James teaches that faith and actions are both important to God.

OUTLINE

James's greetings (1:1)

James was writing to Jewish Christians everywhere.

Endurance (1:2–18)

When life is hard, faith should grow stronger, not weaker.

Hearing and doing the Word of God (1:19 – 2:26)

If we really believe what God says, we will act upon it.

Our words and God's wisdom (3)

The words we speak can help a lot – or hurt a lot. We need God's wisdom to control our words.

Trusting God (4)

We never know what will happen next, but we can trust God to handle it.

General advice on Christian living (5)

Don't trust money more than God. Trust him when life is difficult. Pray and love.

James was one of Jesus' three closest disciples. He was beheaded for his Christian faith by Herod Agrippa about ten years after the death of Jesus.

The busy Damascus Gate gives entry to the Old City of Jerusalem.

A Jewish high priest in his special costume. At the Jerusalem Temple, certain sacrifices had to be offered by the high priest, and he alone could enter the Holiest Place.

Look out for...

As you read through James, look out for...

Direct instructions. *James doesn't play games. He tells Christians exactly what they must do to follow God.*

Evidence of faith. *James tells us how to find out if our faith is true faith – by watching how we live.*

Words. *How we use our words shows a lot about our faith.*

Frequently Asked Questions

Q: Does joy mean a person is laughing and singing when something really bad happens?

A: Joy is not the same as happiness. Happiness is usually the result of a good experience; a fun-filled time. Joy is deeper: it's a peace we have because we know God is in control and with us no matter what happens.

Q: How can a person show faith?

A: No one can live a perfect Christian life. But a person who has faith in Jesus should be trying to live the way God told us to live. A Christian should read God's Word and ask the Holy Spirit for help to do God's will.

Oaths

An oath is when someone calls on God as a witness. The person is saying that God himself would say the same thing because it's true. In Bible times, oaths were taken very seriously. There were simple oaths for everyday use and solemn oaths for important occasions. When swearing an oath, someone might raise his or her hand and say "as sure as the Lord who rescues Israel lives".

An everyday oath today would be saying, "Cross my heart and hope to die." A more solemn oath would be when people testify in court. They raise their hand and put their hand on the Bible and swear or promise to tell "the truth, the whole truth, and nothing but the truth".

James (and Jesus) said we shouldn't take oaths. We should be truthful people, so when we say "yes" or "no" others know we're telling the truth. We should have a reputation for being so honest that no one needs an oath to believe us.

Model of Herod's Temple, Jerusalem. James was leader of the believers in Jerusalem. This Temple was destroyed by the Romans in AD 70.

Study Questions

- How can hard times and problems be good? (1:2–4)
- Why is it important for us to watch what we say? (3:3–12)

1 Peter

Peter wrote this letter to Christians who were being harassed, tortured, and even threatened with their lives because of their faith. He wrote it to encourage them. They were scattered throughout Asia Minor (in modern-day Turkey) and were under pressure for believing in Jesus. Some Christians here had already been killed for their faith in Christ.

Peter spoke from experience. He himself had been beaten and put in prison because he preached about Jesus. He drew comfort from God's love in giving him eternal life. He also knew that being persecuted for his faith strengthened it. God had promised his children eternal life with him in heaven, and that applied to him and to all his Christian readers. So he told them to expect trouble and not to fear it.

This letter was written a long time ago, but many Christians still suffer misunderstanding and ridicule today. Believers in Jesus can learn from Peter how to accept it and look forward to life with Christ in heaven.

OUTLINE

Peter's greetings (1:1–2)

Peter explains who he is and who he is writing to.

Salvation (1:3 – 2:3)

God provided a way of salvation through Jesus. Because we have received that salvation we should live holy lives.

Do what's right (2:4 – 3:12)

Because we're Christians we have a responsibility to do what is right. That means we should be true in our relationships.

Suffering (3:13 – 4:19)

Sometimes we suffer for doing what's right. We still have a responsibility to obey God, even when we're suffering.

Final advice (5)

Peter tells the leaders of the church to be wise and strong.

Peter began his working life as a fisherman, until he was called by Jesus to become a fisher of men.

Persecution

"Persecution" means harassing someone or making someone's life very difficult in any way possible. During Peter's life, the Roman emperor Nero was persecuting Christians all over the Roman Empire.

The persecution happened in a lot of different ways. Sometimes Nero had Christians beaten or put in jail. Sometimes he had them killed. You may have heard stories about Christians being put into an arena with lions. Throughout history, governments and people have hated Christians and hated God. For this reason, Christians have sometimes been persecuted, but through encouragement such as Peter gives, many have stood strong.

The Colosseum, Rome, by night. In this arena, many Christians faced death because of their faith.

Frequently Asked Questions

Q: What good is it if Christians are persecuted for their faith?

A: If Christians live godly lives, their enemies may accuse them of doing evil, but they will bring glory to God in the end.

Q: Why should Christians expect suffering?

A: Christians are followers of Jesus. If he suffered, his followers will suffer too. Many people don't want to be told that Jesus is the only way to God.

Look out for...

As you read through 1 Peter, look out for...

Obeying authority. *Peter talks about authority in the church as well as in the city or nation.*

What Christ has done for us. *In many different ways, Peter tells us what Christ has done for us.*

Suffering. *Christians are being harassed. This is why it's important for Peter to write about suffering.*

Study Questions

- How can Christians grow and mature? (2:1–3)
- How should Christians treat people in authority? (2:13–17)
- What should Christians do about Satan? (5:8–9)

2 Peter

Peter is arrested for belonging to the church. (Acts 12:1–19)

The apostle Peter wrote this second letter to urge Christians to stay close to God. Peter knew he would soon be killed for his beliefs. He wanted to encourage Christians to continue to grow in their faith in Christ.

He told them how important it was to know the Scriptures and to know Christ better and better. Peter pointed out that the Bible is God's Word and is not made up by the people who wrote it down.

Peter also warned against false teachers who would come into the church after he had gone. He said they would deceive people and lead them into sin. Peter didn't want that to happen to his brothers and sisters in Christ. Also, there would be those who denied that Jesus was coming a second time. Peter wanted believers to know that Jesus was delaying his return because God was patient and was giving people time to repent. Meanwhile, Christians should live blameless lives in peace with God and share the gospel with those around them.

OUTLINE

Greetings (1:1)

Peter, like Paul, states who he is (instead of just putting his name at the end of the letter).

Christian growth (1:2–21)

The Bible and faith are important ingredients in growing up.

False teachers (2)

The trouble with false teachers is that they deceive people. But God is never fooled.

End times (3)

The earth won't always keep going just like it is. Life as we know it will change, and God will give us a new heaven and a new earth.

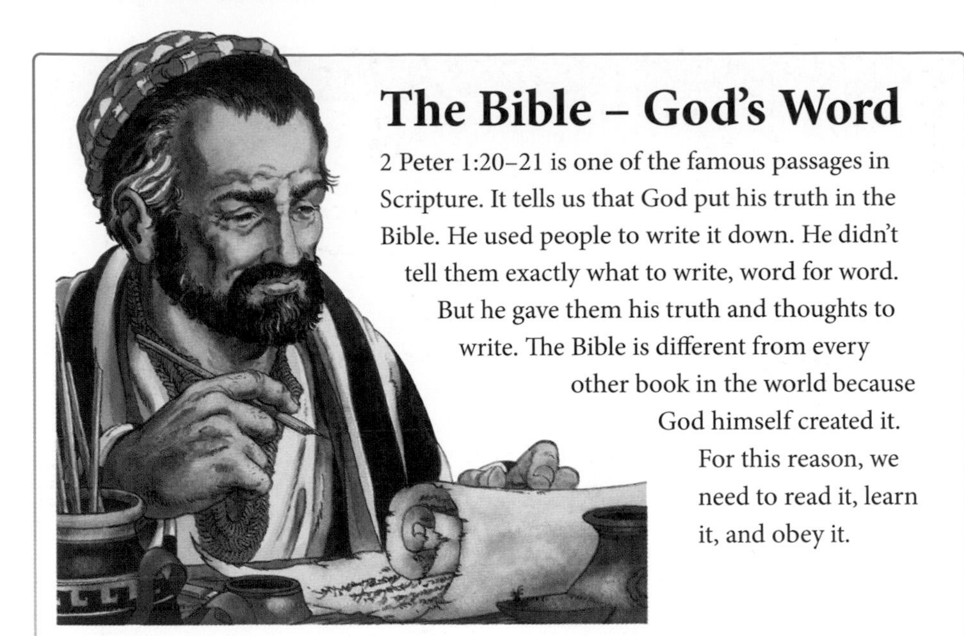

The Bible – God's Word

2 Peter 1:20–21 is one of the famous passages in Scripture. It tells us that God put his truth in the Bible. He used people to write it down. He didn't tell them exactly what to write, word for word. But he gave them his truth and thoughts to write. The Bible is different from every other book in the world because God himself created it. For this reason, we need to read it, learn it, and obey it.

Frequently Asked Questions

Q: What kind of things would false teachers teach?
A: Peter warned that people calling themselves Christians would deny Jesus was Lord. They would blaspheme, live immoral lives, tell others that immorality is OK, and boast.

Q: Why did Peter write about the world blowing up?
A: False teachers were saying that Jesus was not coming back. Peter wanted Christians to know they were wrong. He wrote that one day, Jesus would return and God would create a new home for all his people.

Look out for...

As you read through 2 Peter, look out for...

The ingredients of spiritual growth.
It doesn't happen without effort.

Characteristics of false teachers.
Notice how God will treat them.

Study Questions

- Where did Scripture come from? (1:20–21)
- How does God see time? (3:8–9)
- Since God is going to judge us, how should Christians live? (3:11–13)

1 JOHN

Darkness fell over Jerusalem when Jesus died on the cross. John was an eyewitness of Jesus' life and death.

The apostle John was an eyewitness to the life of Jesus. He'd been there when Jesus was living on earth. He'd heard Jesus with his own ears. He'd seen Jesus with his own eyes. John knew Jesus personally. He knew all about Jesus and the truth about Jesus.

John wrote about this because some people were teaching that Jesus was not really God in human form. They said Jesus was more like a ghost than a real human being. They also said that it didn't matter what people did with their bodies since they would die anyway. These ideas were making Christians wonder if it was all right to sin.

John wanted Christians to know that Jesus is real and really gave them eternal life. John wanted them to know that anyone born into God's family doesn't sin as a way of life. But when Christians do sin, they can ask Jesus to forgive them. He forgives people when they repent, and they can have fellowship with God and with each other. That's the truth about Jesus.

OUTLINE

Jesus is life and light (1)
His lives within us and his light shows us our sin.

Love one another and don't sin (2:1 – 3:24)
When we do not love, we are sinning, because God is love.

False prophets (4:1–6)
A prophet is false if he or she doesn't acknowledge Jesus as the Son of God.

The love of God in us (4:7–21)
God loves us, and that's why we should love each other.

Believe in Jesus (5)
God gives us life through his Son.

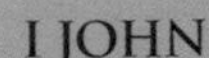

Remains of the Basilica of St John, Ephesus. John likely left Jerusalem and spent his last years in the city of Ephesus.

Frequently Asked Questions

Q: How did John know that Jesus was God as well as a human being?
A: John was with Peter and James when Jesus was transfigured. They saw Jesus' divine glory. They also heard God the Father say that Jesus was his Son.

Q: How did John say people should love fellow humans?
A: John said that love is not just words but also actions. He said that if a Christian friend needs food or clothing, it's not enough to say, "I hope you find food or clothing." You need to give the person food or clothing. Christian love gives help to people in need.

Look out for...

As you read through 1 John, look out for...

Love. *John's love for his readers, God's love for us, and our love for each other.*

Sin. *Its presence and what it causes in our lives.*

Study Questions

- What should a Christian do when he or she sins? (1:9)
- What does "love the world" mean? (2:15–17)
- What does John say Christians will be like when Jesus returns? (3:1–3)

2 JOHN

The shortest book in the Bible can be summed up in two words: truth and love.

The apostle John wrote this short note called 2 John. He warned his dear friend in Christ to beware of those who were not teaching the truth. This special lady probably opened her home to journeying preachers. She was trying to show Christian love and hospitality. But John warned her that not all the teachers and preachers were telling the truth.

There were those who taught that Jesus was not really a human being. They denied the truth of Jesus Christ as God and man. Their teaching was wrong. But if the lady welcomed them, others would think the teachers were wise and listen to them. Then many people would be confused.

If people believe in a Jesus who is not the true Jesus, then they are not really trusting God.

Frequently Asked Question

Q: Why is it important that Jesus is God and man?

A: Two reasons: first, only God is good enough to pay the debt for our sin; second, he needed to be human, so he could show us how to live in God's family here on earth. Jesus is a bridge between us and the heavenly Father.

OUTLINE

Greetings (1:1–3)

John greets a lady – but this may mean a church.

Remain faithful (1:4–6)

Continue to love each other.

Beware of false teachers (1:7–13)

Be careful about people who teach lies.

Look out for...

As you read through 2 John, look out for...

Love. *John always encourages his readers to love one another.*

Strong warnings. *John is outspoken when he talks about false teachers.*

Study Questions

- What is God's definition of love? (1:6)
- Why is 2 John so short? (1:12)

3 JOHN

Journeying teachers and missionaries stayed in the homes of other Christians. One of those Christians was John's friend, Gaius. The apostle John wrote this short letter to Gaius.

John was glad to know that Gaius was staying faithful to Christ. Gaius was sharing his home and belongings with these preachers. It was important to John that Christians helped their fellow Christians. John didn't want the missionaries to be in need.

Another man in the church was refusing to help the missionaries. His name was Diotrephes. He wouldn't let others help them either. John told Gaius not to follow Diotrephes' bad example.

OUTLINE

Greetings (1:1–2)
From John to Gaius.

Good job! (1:3–8)
Gaius has been very hospitable to journeying preachers.

Diotrephes (1:9–10)
Diotrephes was saying bad things about the apostles and causing trouble in the church.

Choose good examples (1:11–15)
Demetrius is trustworthy and a good example for Gaius to follow.

Look out for...

As you read through 3 John, look out for...

Hospitality. *John compliments Gaius for looking after journeying preachers and missionaries.*

Frequently Asked Question

Q: Why didn't John want the non-believers to help the missionaries?
A: John didn't want non-believers to think the missionaries and Christian teachers were just trying to get money for themselves.

Study Questions

- How did John show that our bodies and our spirits are important to God? (1:2)
- What gave John joy? (It would probably give your parents joy too!) (1:4)

JUDE

Jude warns that false teachers are like "trees that have been pulled up by the roots and are completely dead". (1:12, GNB)

OUTLINE

Greetings (1:1–2)
Jude greets all Christians.

False teachers (1:3–19)
Jude reminds his readers that God hated sin in the past and still does.

Strong faith (1:20–25)
Jude encourages Christians to stick to what they know is right, no matter what.

Ever since the beginning of the church, Christians have had to beware of false teachers. Jude wrote this book to warn believers that false teaching could lead to sad results.

Jude was a brother of James and a half-brother of Jesus. Like James, at first he didn't believe Jesus was the Messiah. But after Jesus rose from the dead, Jude believed.

Jude's main concern was false teachers. They were saying Christians could do whatever they wanted because of God's freely given love. They said Christians didn't have to obey any authority.

Instead, Jude reminded Christians to stay close to Christ, and to love and obey him. He also said they should help others understand God's truth, so they could be saved too.

Jude was not trying to scare anybody. He closed his letter with the great promise that Jesus is able to keep us from falling. He praised Jesus for his majesty, power, and authority.

Frequently Asked Question

Q: Doesn't the Bible teach that God will forgive any sin?

A: God does forgive any sin. But he doesn't want people to live in sin. He wants us to turn to him and trust in Jesus Christ. Then he gives us power to turn from our sin.

Sodom and Gomorrah

Jude refers to an Old Testament story about two towns, Sodom and Gomorrah (Genesis 18–19). God told Abraham he was going to destroy these towns because of their wickedness. Abraham's nephew, Lot, lived there, so Abraham asked God to spare the cities if he could find just ten righteous people there. But he couldn't even find ten.

God told Lot's family not to look back as they left. The town burned to the ground. Unfortunately Lot's wife disobeyed God and looked back at her burning home – and turned into a pillar of salt.

To this day, as in Jude's day, Sodom and Gomorrah remind us that God judges sin.

Look out for...

As you read through Jude, look out for...

Punishment of sin. *Jude spends much time telling us about sinful people and how God punished them.*

Christian life. *Jude closes with a great description of the Christian life.*

A rabbi holds up the precious Torah scroll in the synagogue.

Study Question

- How will it be when we see the Lord? (1:24–25)

Revelation

Revelation is the only book of prophecy in the New Testament. It's also called the "Apocalypse", or disclosure. It includes promises of blessing to those who read, hear, and keep the words of Revelation.

The apostle John wrote Revelation when he was very old. He was exiled on the island of Patmos because he refused to stop preaching about Jesus. Jesus gave John this vision to tell Christians what was going to happen. Jesus gave special messages to seven different churches in Asia. Jesus commended the churches for their strengths and criticized them for their failings. Then he told them how to correct their problems. These same problems exist today. Christians can learn from Jesus' words to these churches.

The book of Revelation is filled with picture language. It tells how unbelievers will fight against Jesus and against God's people. It urges believers to stay true to Jesus and not to believe Satan's lies. And in the end, it tells of Christ's great victory.

The joy of being with Jesus in heaven for all eternity far outweighs the difficulties we will have on earth.

A beach on the small Greek island of Patmos, where John was in exile.

Visions

John describes events in heaven by comparing them with things we have seen on earth. These are his "visions". Many visions are mentioned in the Bible. Jacob saw a vision of angels going up and down stairs that led to heaven (Genesis 28:10–15). Ezekiel saw many visions. In the first chapter of his book, he describes a vision of a windstorm and creatures that looked like men with wings and with feet like calves. Daniel also had many visions. Some of Ezekiel's and Daniel's visions had to do with the last days of the earth, just as John's did.

Revelation describes visions of horses and riders. It has many visions. These visions give us a glimpse into the future, but when it all really happens it will be like nothing we have ever seen before.

Frequently Asked Questions

Q: What were the things for which Jesus commended the churches?

A: Jesus commended the churches for hard work, for suffering persecution and poverty, for being true to the faith, for love and service, and for being effective.

Q: What things were they doing that he didn't like?

A: Jesus criticized the churches for forgetting their first love, for compromise, for immorality, for being superficial, and for being "lukewarm". But the churches at Smyrna and Philadelphia got nothing but praise from Jesus.

OUTLINE

Jesus is coming back (1)

John describes his vision of Jesus returning.

Seven letters to seven churches (2–3)

John writes to seven churches, telling them good things and bad things about the way they are serving God.

Vision of the end of earth as it is now (4–19)

John's visions include scrolls, trumpets, creatures we have never seen, angels, plagues, a wedding banquet, and horses.

The end of time (20–22)

John describes Satan's final punishment, the new earth and the new heaven.

Remains of the city of Laodicea, one of the places that John wrote a letter to, included in the book of Revelation.

Look out for...

As you read through Revelation, look out for...

Messages to the churches. *There are seven messages for seven specific churches.*

Signs of the times. *John gives us many clues about what will happen when Christ comes back and sets up his new kingdom.*

Study Questions

- What awful punishment awaits those who worship the beast? (14:9–11)
- What will eternity with God be like? (21:1 – 22:7)

Big Ideas in the Bible

Ascension: Jesus' return to heaven after his death and resurrection.

Atonement: Payment for sin. Jesus' death atoned for all our sins.

Baptism: A sign that a person is a follower of Christ. Some churches pour water over the person's head; others dip the person under the water. Some churches only baptize people when they are old enough to understand baptism. Some churches baptize babies when their parents request it.

Beatitudes: A word meaning "blessings". Part of Jesus' Sermon on the Mount describes what makes people blessed.

Birthright: The legal right to be the leader of the family and to get a double amount of the inheritance when the father dies. Jacob traded a bowl of stew for his brother Esau's birthright.

The Sea of Galilee viewed from near the "Mount of Beatitudes".

Bless: To pray God's best for someone; to wish the person well; to speak well of the person.

Book of Life: The record of those who trust in Christ and will live in heaven with him.

Born again: To be born spiritually by trusting in Christ's death and resurrection.

Confess: To admit your sins; to say publicly what you believe.

Covenant: A promise or agreement between two or more people. God made a covenant with Abraham. God promised to bless the whole world through Abraham's descendants.

Cross: The place where the Romans executed Jesus; a symbol of Jesus' great love in taking away our sins.

Dedicate: To set something aside for God. Hannah dedicated Samuel to God before he was born.

Eternal life: The new life Jesus gives people when they trust in him. Eternal life begins immediately and goes on through eternity.

Faith: Complete trust in God that he exists and that what he says in the Bible is true. Obeying God.

Forgive: To pardon or cancel a debt; to wipe the record clean. When people place their trust in Jesus, God forgives their sin.

Fruit of the Spirit: The result in people's lives when they let the Holy Spirit have control. The fruit is love, joy, peace, patience, kindness, goodness, faithfulness, gentleness, and self-control. (Galatians 5:22–23)

Palm crosses, often distributed at Easter to remind believers of Palm Sunday and Good Friday.

Glorification: The promise that Christians will be like Jesus when he takes them home to heaven. (1 John 3:2–3)

Grace: God's free gift of forgiveness and salvation.

Holiness: Purity; being completely without sin. God is holy.

Justification: God regarding us as sinless even though we're not. He does this for every person who trusts in Jesus.

Mercy: God's goodness to us, even though we don't deserve it.

Redemption: The work that Jesus did on the cross: he paid the debt, or price, for our sin.

Repentance: Turning away from sin to God.

Resurrection: Rising from the dead. Jesus rose three days after he was crucified. Believers who die before Jesus returns will be resurrected at his second coming.

Salvation: God's free gift of forgiveness from sin and a new life in Christ. Everyone is a sinner, but Christ's death on the cross paid the penalty for our sin. Each person who trusts in Christ for forgiveness receives salvation.

Sin: Going against God's will; disobeying God; doing wrong. Every person sins.

Soul, spirit: The emotions, mind, and personality of a person; what lives on after the body dies.

Temptation: Wanting to do wrong, to sin.

Unbelief: Refusing to believe in God or his Word; the opposite of faith.

Promises in the Bible

Promises made to believers

A rainbow, reminding us of God's promise to Noah.

- **A full life**
  John 10:10
- **A crown of life**
  Revelation 2:10
- **A home in heaven**
  John 14:1–3
- **Answered prayer**
  1 John 5:14
- **A sure hope for the future**
  2 Timothy 1:12
- **Cleansing**
  John 15:3
- **Comfort**
  Isaiah 51:3
- **God's deliverance**
  2 Timothy 4:18
- **Everlasting life**
  John 3:16
- **Gifts of the Spirit**
  1 Corinthians 12
- **God's care**
  1 Peter 5:6–7
- **Growth in the Christian life**
  Ephesians 4:11–15
- **God's guidance**
  Isaiah 42:16
- **Hope**
  Hebrews 6:18–19
- **Joy**
  Isaiah 35:10
- **Peace**
  John 14:27
- **Rest**
  Hebrews 4:9, 11
- **Resurrection**
  Romans 8:11
- **Spiritual light**
  John 12:46
- **Strength**
  Philippians 4:13
- **Understanding**
  Psalm 119:104
- **Victory**
  1 John 5:4
- **Wisdom**
  James 1:5

Fifty Very Important Passages

The Bible is a very big book. Here are some of its most important passages.

- **Creation**
  Genesis 1
- **The first sin**
  Genesis 3
- **Noah and the flood**
  Genesis 6 – 9:17
- **The tower of Babel**
  Genesis 11:1–9
- **Abraham and Isaac**
  Genesis 22:1–19
- **Esau and Jacob**
  Genesis 25:19–34; 27
- **The story of Joseph**
  Genesis 37–50
- **Baby Moses**
  Exodus 2:1–10
- **The Exodus**
  Exodus 7–14
- **The Ten Commandments**
  Exodus 20
- **Jericho is captured**
  Joshua 6:15–21
- **Gideon's little army**
  Judges 7:15–23
- **The story of Samson**
  Judges 13–16
- **The story of Ruth**
  Book of Ruth
- **The boy Samuel**
  1 Samuel 1–3
- **David kills Goliath**
  1 Samuel 17
- **The shepherd psalm**
  Psalm 23
- **The fiery furnace**
  Daniel 3
- **Daniel in the lions' den**
  Daniel 6
- **The story of Jonah**
  Book of Jonah
- **The birth of Jesus**
  Luke 2
- **John the Baptist preaches**
  Matthew 3:1–12
- **Young Jesus in the Temple**
  Luke 2:41–52
- **The baptism of Jesus**
  Matthew 3:13–17; John 1:31–34
- **Jesus is tempted**
  Matthew 4:1–11; Luke 4:1–13
- **The Sermon on the Mount**
  Matthew 5–7
- **The Lord's Prayer**
  Matthew 6:9–13; Luke 11:2–4
- **The woman at the well**
  John 4:1–42
- **Becoming fishers of men**
  Matthew 4:18–22; Luke 5:1–11
- **A centurion's faith**
  Matthew 8:5–13; Luke 7:1–10
- **The story of the sower**
  Matthew 13:1–23; Mark 4:1–20
- **The true vine**
  John 15
- **The prodigal son**
  Luke 15:11–32
- **Jesus is transfigured**
  Matthew 17:1–13; Mark 9:2–13
- **Mary and Martha**
  Luke 10:38–42
- **Zacchaeus**
  Luke 19:1–10
- **Mary anoints Jesus**
  Mark 14:3–9; John 12:1–8
- **The Last Supper**
  Matthew 26:17–30; Mark 14:12–26
- **Jesus is betrayed**
  Mark 14:10–11; Luke 22:1–6; John 18:1–11
- **Death and resurrection of Jesus**
  Matthew 27–28; Mark 15–16; Luke 23 – 24:12; John 19:16 – 20:10
- **The risen Christ**
  Luke 24:35–49; John 20:19–23
- **Doubting Thomas**
  John 20:24–29
- **The Great Commission**
  Matthew 28:16–20
- **The Holy Spirit comes**
  Acts 2
- **Conversion of Saul**
  Acts 9:1–19
- **Peter is rescued from prison**
  Acts 12:1–19
- **Paul's missionary travels**
  Acts 13–21
- **Living for God**
  Romans 12
- **Love**
  1 Corinthians 13
- **The future**
  Revelation 21:1–8

Who's Who in the Bible
Old Testament

Adam and Eve
Adam and Eve are the parents of the human race. God created them to live in the Garden of Eden and be his friends. Eve disobeyed God and persuaded Adam to join her. Because they sinned, God sent them out of the garden. Sickness and death entered the world.

(Genesis 1:26 – 5:5)

Noah
Noah and his family were the only people God saved from the flood. God told Noah to build a huge boat and fill it with food for his family and with animals of every kind.

(Genesis 5:29 – 10:32)

This view of Noah's ark gives some indication of its massive dimensions.

Abraham and Sarah
Abraham and Sarah were the father and mother of God's people, the Jews. God promised Abraham that he would have more children than the stars in the sky. Abraham and Sarah were old and still had no children. Finally, God gave them a son named Isaac. God tested Abraham's faith many times. But Abraham trusted God.

(Genesis 11–25)

Isaac and Rebekah
Isaac was the son of Abraham and Sarah – the son God had promised them. He married Rebekah and God gave them twin sons. Rebekah told Jacob, the

younger, to trick his father, Isaac, so he would get the family leadership. Jacob had to run away from Esau, his angry brother.

(Genesis 17:15 – 35:29)

Jacob and Rachel

Jacob the trickster was tricked by his uncle Laban into marrying Leah. Jacob had to work many years to marry Rachel, who he loved. God changed Jacob's name to Israel. His sons and two grandsons became the twelve tribes of Israel.

(Genesis 25–50)

Joseph

Joseph was Jacob's best-loved son. His jealous brothers plotted to kill him, but instead sold him into slavery. Joseph became the trusted slave of an Egyptian leader. Later, he was accused of crimes, put in prison, and forgotten. Finally, Joseph was called to tell the meaning of a dream Pharaoh had. Overnight, Joseph became second to Pharaoh in all of Egypt! Because of famine, Joseph's brothers went to Egypt to buy food. They didn't recognize their brother. He tested them. When he found they were sorry for what they'd done, he told them he was Joseph.

(Genesis 30–50)

Moses

Moses was a Hebrew who grew up in Egypt, escaped to the desert, and returned to free God's people from slavery. The Egyptians didn't want to lose their slaves, but after God sent ten plagues, they finally let them go. Moses had a hard time leading the stubborn people. They often disobeyed God. The short trip to the Promised Land became a forty-year journey. Moses was a strong leader who loved God and his people.

(Exodus, Leviticus, Numbers, and Deuteronomy)

Joshua

God chose Joshua to take Moses' place when he died. He was one of the twelve spies who went into the Promised Land. Joshua led the people into the Promised Land and into the battle of Jericho.

(Deuteronomy 1:22–40; Joshua 1–24)

Ruth

Ruth was not an Israelite; she was from the land of Moab. Her people prayed to idols, not to the true God. But Ruth married an Israelite in Moab. He, his brothers, and his father died. Naomi, Ruth's mother-in-law, was returning to Bethlehem. Ruth chose to go with Naomi and follow God. Ruth took care of her mother-in-law. Then God gave Ruth a new husband, Boaz. God gave them a son named Obed, who was the grandfather of King David.

(Ruth 1–4)

Samuel

Samuel was a prophet and priest of the people of Israel. From boyhood, Samuel lived with Eli, the high priest. Samuel became a spiritual leader of his people and was the priest who anointed Saul as king, and later, David too.

(1 Samuel 1–28)

Saul

Saul was the first king of Israel. At first, he obeyed God. Later, he disobeyed God and Samuel said God would give the kingdom to someone else. Saul continued to reign for forty years. During much of that time, he chased David and tried to kill him. David waited patiently for God to give him the kingdom. Saul and his sons were killed on the same day in a battle with the Philistines.

(1 Samuel 9–31)

David

David was the best-known king of Israel. He became king after Saul was killed. The people loved David. That made Saul jealous.

For many years before he became king, David had to run away from Saul. David was an excellent soldier. He learned his fighting skills from his years as a shepherd, fighting off lions and bears. That's how he killed the powerful giant Goliath.

David was also a musician and poet. He played the harp and wrote many of the psalms. People use his prayers and praise songs to worship God today.

David loved God, but he still sinned. He was truly sorry and asked God to forgive him. God called David "a man after my own heart" (Acts 13:22).

(1 Samuel 16–31; 2 Samuel 1–24; 1 Kings 1–2)

Solomon

Solomon is known as the wisest man who ever lived. Solomon was the son of King David and Bathsheba. He was the third king of Israel. God allowed Solomon to build the Temple in Jerusalem where the Jewish people met with God. It was famous for its beauty.

Solomon wrote many proverbs, some psalms, the book of Ecclesiastes, and the Song of Songs in the Old Testament.

In spite of his wisdom, Solomon disobeyed God in a very important matter. He married many wives from foreign countries who brought with them their idols. God divided Solomon's kingdom after he died.

(2 Samuel 12:24 – 24:25; 1 Kings 1:1 – 11:43)

Elijah

Elijah was a prophet so close to God that he never died; God took him straight to heaven! God let Elijah do many important miracles. Elijah declared that there would be no rain until he said so. Famine resulted. God used Elijah to bring a dead boy back to life.

Elijah took a bold stand against the prophets of Baal. King Ahab and Queen Jezebel were supporting Baal-worship. Elijah challenged all the prophets of Baal to prove who was the real God. Nothing happened when the priests of Baal prayed to their god. When Elijah prayed to the Lord, God answered immediately!

(1 Kings 17:1 – 22:53; 2 Kings 1:1 – 2:11)

Ezra

Ezra was a faithful Jewish priest while he was a captive in Persia. King Artaxerxes allowed him to take other captives back to Jerusalem. They took things they needed to worship the Lord.

Ezra studied God's Law and taught the people, so they could repent and turn back to God.

(Ezra 1–10)

Esther

Esther is the second woman with a book of the Bible named after her. Esther was a young Jewish woman whom God used to save her people from all being killed. She became queen to King Xerxes. A palace official plotted to kill all the Jews in Persia. Queen Esther was able to expose the plan and save the Jews.

The Jewish holiday Purim is still celebrated in memory of that victory.

(Esther 1–10)

Job

Job is known for his patience. God allowed Satan to take away Job's wealth, family, and finally his health. Satan said Job served God only because he had an easy life. But God knew Job loved him and not just the things God gave to him. Job didn't understand why he was having so much trouble. Job's friends said he'd done something wrong. Finally, Job realized God was yet more powerful than he had thought. God gave Job new wealth and a new family.

(Job 1–42)

Isaiah

Isaiah was an Israelite who became a prophet when he saw a vision of the Lord in heaven. It made him very aware of his sinfulness to see God in all his holiness. But God forgave him and Isaiah was never the same after that. He faithfully preached that God was going to judge his people – but there was hope. Many of his prophecies are about the Messiah.

(Isaiah 1–66)

Jeremiah

Jeremiah is often called the weeping prophet. He warned his people about punishment that would come to them from God, but they did not listen to him. They accused him of being a traitor. He was mocked and abused for giving God's message, but he did not give up. Jeremiah was taken away into captivity along with the people from Jerusalem. He is called the weeping prophet because no one ever listened to him and all the bad things happened that God said would happen.

(Jeremiah 1–52; Lamentations 1–5)

Daniel

Daniel was a young Jewish man who became an adviser to four Babylonian kings while an exile in Babylonia. He prayed to God faithfully in Babylon even when his life was on the line. Once he was put into a den of hungry lions because he prayed to God. But God protected him and kept him alive.

God gave Daniel the ability to tell the meaning of dreams. He also prophesied about the end times.

(Daniel 1–12)

Jonah

Jonah was the prophet who tried to run away from God. He did not want to tell the wicked people of Nineveh to turn to God because he knew that God would forgive them if they did. It took a storm at sea and a rescue by a huge fish for Jonah to change his mind. He finally did what he was supposed to. But he never got over the fact that the people listened and were forgiven.

(Jonah 1–4)

New Testament

Mary

Mary, a young Jewish virgin, was chosen by God to bear his son, Jesus Christ, by the power of the Holy Spirit. The angel Gabriel announced this to her in Nazareth. Mary stood at the foot of the cross as Jesus died, and Jesus told the apostle John to look after her. She was also in the upper room on the day of Pentecost.

(Matthew 1; Mark 6:3; Luke 1–2; John 2:1–11; 19:25–27; Acts 1)

John the Baptist

John the Baptist, son of Elizabeth and Zechariah, lived in the Judean wilderness. He wore clothes of camels' hair, as the prophet Elijah had done centuries earlier. He preached repentance, paving the way for his cousin, Jesus, whom he baptized in the River Jordan. John was imprisoned, and later beheaded, by Herod.

(Matthew 3; 11:1–19; 14:1–12; Mark 1:1–8; Luke 1; John 1:1–34)

Andrew

Andrew introduced his brother, Peter, to Jesus on the shores of Lake Galilee, where they, John, and James fished. Andrew brought to Jesus a boy who had two fish and five loaves, which Jesus used to feed 5,000 people.

(Matthew 4:18–20; Mark 1:16–18; John 1:35–42; 6:8–9)

Peter

Peter always heads the lists of the apostles. With his brother, Andrew, Peter left his fishing and became one of Jesus' three closest disciples. At Caesarea Philippi, he told Jesus he was "the Christ, the Son of the living God". Peter led the first Christians, preaching fearlessly from the day of Pentecost, when 3,000 people were baptized. Peter wrote two short letters, and much of Mark's Gospel is likely a summary of his teaching. It is thought he was executed by Nero in Rome.

(Matthew 4:18–20; 10:2; 14:25–31; 16:13–23; 17:1–13; 26:31–35, 69–75; 1 and 2 Peter)

Peter denies Jesus.

James

James was a fisherman, working with his brother, John, and father, Zebedee. Jesus called him, and he followed at once. Jesus gave John and James the nickname 'sons of thunder'. James became one of Jesus' three closest apostles, whom Jesus chose to have with him at special moments, such as the transfiguration. James was beheaded for his Christian faith by Herod Agrippa I, about ten years after the death of Jesus.

(Matthew 4:21–22; 10:2; 17:1–13; 26:37; Mark 5:37; 10:35–45; Luke 9:51–56; Acts 12:2)

John

John, a fisherman and son of Zebedee, was one of Jesus' inner circle of three apostles. John, who leaned on Jesus at the Last Supper, was Jesus' closest friend, and as Jesus was dying, he asked John to look after Mary, his mother. John wrote one Gospel, the book of Revelation, during his exile on the island of Patmos, and three short letters. In his

Gospel, John never mentions himself by name, but uses the words 'the disciple Jesus loved' instead. He became a leader in the early church.

(Matthew 4:21–22; 10:2; 20:20–23; John 13:23–25; 19:25–27; Acts 1:13; 3–4; Galatians 2:9; 1, 2, and 3 John; Revelation 1:1)

Matthew

Matthew, also known as Levi, was called from being a tax collector to follow Jesus. He abandoned everything and held a feast in his house for Jesus and many tax collectors and sinners. He is the author of the first Gospel.

(Matthew 9:9–10)

Thomas

At the Last Supper, Thomas asked Jesus, "How can we know the way?" and Jesus replied, "I am the way, the truth and the life." Thomas is remembered as "doubting" Thomas because he said he would never believe in Jesus' resurrection unless he saw Jesus and touched his wounds. When the risen Lord Jesus did appear to him, Thomas immediately called him his Lord and God.

(Matthew 10:3; John 11:16; 14:5–6; 20:24–28)

Philip

Philip was a fisherman from Bethsaida, who brought Nathanael (Bartholomew) to meet Jesus. At the Last Supper, Philip asked Jesus to show them the Father, and Jesus replied, 'I am in the Father and the Father is in me.'

(John 1:43–51; 6:5–7; 12:20–22; 14:8–9)

Judas Iscariot

Judas Iscariot was the treasurer for the twelve apostles. For thirty silver pieces he betrayed Jesus in the garden of Gethsemane. Judas was later overtaken by remorse, returned the silver and hanged himself.

(Matthew 26:1 – 27:10; Acts 1:15–26)

Mary Magdalene

Mary was named Magdalene after the town she came from, Magdala. Jesus drove seven demons from her and she became his follower, standing close to his cross when he died. Mary Magdalene was the first person Jesus appeared to after his resurrection.

(Matthew 27:55–56; 28:1–10; Mark 15:40; 16:1–8; Luke 8:2; John 19:25; 20:1–18)

John Mark

Mark, or John Mark, writer of the second Gospel, lived in Jerusalem, where the first Christians met in his mother's house. Mark, cousin of Barnabas, accompanied Paul and Barnabas on their first missionary journey, but he left them halfway, and Paul refused to take him on his second trip. Later Mark joined Paul in Rome, and was described by Paul as 'my son Mark'. Mark's Gospel is based on Peter's account of Jesus' life to John Mark.

(Mark; Acts 12–15; 2 Timothy 4; Philemon)

Mary

Mary, the sister of Martha and Lazarus, loved to sit at Jesus' feet and listen to his teaching. A short time before Jesus' death, she anointed his feet with perfume.

(Mark 14:3–9; Luke 10:38–42; John 11:1 – 12:8)

Martha

With her sister, Mary, and brother, Lazarus, Martha often entertained Jesus in her home in Bethany, near Jerusalem. Martha once complained to Jesus that Mary just sat and listened to Jesus while she did all the work. Jesus replied that Mary had chosen what was better.

(Luke 10:38–42; John 11:1 – 12:8)

Luke

A Greek-speaking doctor who wrote the third Gospel, Luke was also a friend of Paul. He accompanied the apostle on some of his journeys, and recorded his experiences in the book of Acts. Luke sailed to Rome with Paul, staying with him while he was a prisoner there.

(Luke; Acts; Colossians 4; 2 Timothy 4)

Zacchaeus

Zacchaeus, a wealthy, cheating tax collector, climbed a tree to see Jesus as he passed through Jericho. Jesus told him to come down and then went to his house. Afterwards, Zacchaeus called Jesus "Lord" and said he would give half his money to the poor.

(Luke 19)

Nicodemus

Nicodemus was a Jewish religious leader who went to talk with Jesus at night. He asked Jesus many questions, but did not really understand at first. Later on, he tried to stand up for Jesus in the religious meetings. The other leaders made fun of him. After Jesus was crucified, Nicodemus helped Joseph of Arimathea bury Jesus. By then, he understood that Jesus is God's Son.

(John 3:1–21; 7:50–52; 19:39–40)

Barnabas

Barnabas was a Christian leader in the early church. His name means "son of encouragement". The apostles called him this because he was always helping people. He sold a piece of property and gave the money to help the needy.

Barnabas journeyed with Paul, taking the gospel to people who had not heard about Jesus.

(Acts 4:36–37; 9:27 – 15:39)

Stephen

Stephen was the leader of seven deacons the Jerusalem church chose to look after poor widows. Some Jews objected to Stephen's preaching. When he accused them of killing Jesus Christ, they stoned him to death. Stephen was the first Christian martyr. His death was witnessed by Saul (Paul).

(Acts 6:1 – 8:2)

Stephen is tried by the Jewish religious court.

Philip

Philip, along with Stephen, was one of seven deacons appointed by the Jerusalem church. He became a leading evangelist among the Samaritans and Gentiles, and told a visiting Ethiopian official the Good News about Jesus, which resulted in the man's baptism.

(Acts 6:5; 8:4–13, 26–40; 21:8)

Paul

Paul was a missionary, preacher, and writer of Scripture. God changed him from a man who hated Jesus and his followers to one of Jesus' most devoted followers. He took three missionary journeys to take the gospel to places all over the Roman Empire.

People did not always like what he had to say. Paul was beaten, stoned, imprisoned, and harassed many times because of his love for Christ.

Paul wrote thirteen of the New Testament books: Romans, 1 Corinthians, 2 Corinthians, Galatians, Ephesians, Philippians, Colossians, 1 Thessalonians, 2 Thessalonians, 1 Timothy, 2 Timothy, Titus, and Philemon.

(Acts 7:58 – 28:31 and the letters Paul wrote)

Silas

A leader of the church in Jerusalem, Silas went with Paul on his second missionary journey, and was jailed with him at Philippi. Silas is probably the same as "Silvanus", mentioned in Paul's letters, and who helped Peter write his first letters.

(Acts 15–18; 2 Corinthians 1; 1 Thessalonians 1; 1 Peter 5)

Timothy

Timothy was like a son to the apostle Paul. He went on missionary journeys with Paul. Paul also sent Timothy to help churches solve problems. Timothy served some of these churches as pastor.

Paul wrote two letters to Timothy, encouraging and instructing him in his duties. Timothy may have been with Paul when he died.

(Acts 16:1–5; Romans 16:21; Philippians 1:1)

Aquila and Priscilla

Aquila and Priscilla were a husband and wife team who worked and journeyed with Paul. They were Jewish Christians from Rome who helped others understand the gospel. They opened their home as a church and made their living making tents.

(Acts 18; Romans 16:3–5; 1 Corinthians 16:19)

Index

A

B

C

D

E

F

G

H

I

J

K

L

M

N

O

P

R

S

T

U

V

W

Z

Acknowledgments

Text acknowledgments

Unless otherwise indicated, all Scripture quotations are taken from the Holy Bible, New Living Translation, copyright © 1996, 2004, 2007 by Tyndale House Foundation. Used by permission of Tyndale House Publishers, Inc., Carol Stream, Illinois 60188. All rights reserved.

Scripture quotations marked CEV are taken from the Contemporary English Version. Copyright © 1991, 1992, 1995 by American Bible Society. Used by permission.

Scripture quotations marked GNB are taken from the Good News Bible © 1994 published by the Bible Societies/HarperCollins Publishers Ltd UK, Good News Bible © American Bible Society 1966, 1971, 1976, 1992. Used with permission.

Scripture quotations marked TLB are taken from The Living Bible copyright © 1971. Used by permission of Tyndale House Publishers, Inc., Carol Stream, Illinois 60188. All rights reserved.

Scripture quotations marked NIV are taken from the Holy Bible, New International Version®, NIV®. Copyright © 1973, 1978, 1984, 2011 by Biblica, Inc.™ Used by permission of Zondervan. All rights reserved worldwide. www.zondervan.com The "NIV" and "New International Version" are trademarks registered in the United States Patent and Trademark Office by Biblica, Inc.™

Picture acknowledgments

Every effort has been made to trace and contact copyright owners. We apologize for any omissions or errors.

Illustrations

Fred Apps: pp. 22, 28, 72, 86, 90, 94, 99, 105, 120, 203, 228 (lion)

Shirley Bellwood: pp. 204, 215

Martin Bustamente: pp. 3/60–61/back cover, 3/88–89/back cover, 3/162–63/back cover, 64–65, 140–41/front cover inset, 144–45, 164–65, 170–71, 172–73

Bill Corbett: pp. 15/back gatefold, 26–27, 52–53/back cover, 134–35, 156–57/front gatefold, 180–81, 224

Peter Dennis: pp. 3/7, 3/179/front cover inset, 47/spine, 69 (bottom), 103, 110, 115, 143, 179, 192, 196, 217

Jeremy Gower: p. 44

Donald Harley: pp. 112 (top), 125, 187, 201

Alan Harris: pp. 29, 102

James Macdonald: p. 199

Tony Morris: pp. 136–37, 150–51

Alan Parry: pp. 24, 77, 91, 202

Alan Parry/© Bill Noller International Publishing, San Dimas, CA. 91773: pp. 10, 14, 18 (bottom), 20, 21, 33, 34, 35, 41 (bottom), 42, 43, 50, 56, 57, 66, 83, 98, 116, 118, 149 (top), 152, 155, 158, 169, 194, 208, 209, 210

Claudia Saraceni: p. 124

Richard Scott: pp. 3/front cover inset (shadow of cross), 18 (top), 19, 23, 38, 40, 41 (top), 46 (both), 54, 58, 59, 69 (top), 74, 80, 85, 96, 97, 101, 112 (bottom), 128, 129, 130, 131/main cover illustration, 132, 133, 147 (both), 149 (bottom), 176, 198, 206, 225–27, 228 (Daniel), 229–31

Photographs

Amsterdam Bible Museum: p. 49

AWL: pp. 28, 117, 172 (Temple of Apollo) and 177 (main photo) Jon Arnold

Dreamstime: pp. 3/100/back cover Vadil; 25 Hsandler; 33 Jeppo75; 68 Ivanderbiesen; 75 Featurecars; 82 (main photo) Orientaly; 85 Boggy; 95 (top) Neilneil; 104 Gofer; 108 Diomedes66; 111 Javax; 148 Renewer; 153 Orcearo; 167 Cdcramer; 168, 207 Timehacker; 175 (main photo) Nikolais; 182 Philcold; 184 (top), 188 (main photo) Karapas; 185 (main photo) Oez; 197 Yurok; 199 Verityjohnson; 205 Compuinfoto; 211 Evrenkalinbacak; 214 (main photo) Roboriginal; 216–17 Stockbksts; 220 Majeczka; 221 Nigel Monckton; 222 Yakobchuk Vasiliy; front cover inset (Crete) Maigi

Israel Government Tourist Office: pp. 12, 32 (top), 41, 43, 47, 71, 78, 121, 123, 162, 204

John McRay: pp. 183 (main photo), 190 (main photo)

Lion Hudson plc: pp. 14, 19, 21, 23, 34 (header), 38, 50, 54 (header), 57, 59, 66, 69, 72, 74 (header), 77, 80, 82 (header), 90, 92 (header), 93, 94, 96, 99, 103, 107 (header), 110, 112, 114 (header), 116 (header), 118, 120, 122 (header), 142, 147, 152, 158, 166 (header), 172 (header), 175 (header), 177 (header), 190 (header), 191, 192, 194, 198, 200, 203, 206, 208, 210, 212, 213, 214 (header), 216 (header)

Tim Dowley Associates: pp. 3/107/front cover inset (Nineveh gate), 3/back cover (Capernaum synagogue), 3 (St Catherine's Monastery), 5, 30, 31, 32 (cup and plate), 34 (bottom), 54 (main photo), 67, 74 (main photo), 76, 79, 81, 84, 86, 92 (main photo), 95 (bottom), 97, 101, 105, 106, 107, 113, 114 (main photo), 119, 122 (bottom), 132, 138, 146, 166 (main photo), 178, 180, 183 (header), 184 (bottom), 185 (header), 188 (header), 193, 196, 219

Zev Radovan: pp. 70, 87, 116 (Baal)